EATING
LAS VEGAS

EATING
LAS VEGAS

THE 52 ESSENTIAL
RESTAURANTS

John Curtas

HUNTINGTON PRESS
LAS VEGAS, NEVADA

EATING LAS VEGAS
The 52 Essential Restaurants

Published by
Huntington Press
3665 Procyon Street
Las Vegas, NV 89103
Phone (702) 252-0655
e-mail: books@huntingtonpress.com

Copyright ©2020, John Curtas

ISBN: 978-1-944877-39-2
$15.95US

Production & Design: Laurie Cabot, Tanya Maynard

Cover Photo: Verti Cucina/Palms

Inside Photos: Spoon ©Torsten Schon, Dreamstime.com

Anthony Mair: x, 36; é by José Andrés: xi; Emily Watson: 8; Chris Wessling: 20, 30; Aria at CityCenter: 22; Ryan Forebes: 24; Station Casinos: 26, 170, 173; Bouchon: 28; John Curtas: 32, 54, 68, 140, 142, 143, 149, 150, 151, 152, 154, 158, 159, 166, 177, 183, 187, 188, 189, 196, 197, 204, 206, 207, 210, 211; Cipriani/Danielle DeBruno: 34; District One: 38; Beverly Poppe: 40; Sabin Orr: 42, 76, 94, 108; Louiie Victa: 44, 90; Elia Authentic Greek Taverna: 46; Eric Gladstone: 48, 181; Cosmopolitan of Las Vegas: 50; Vox Communication: 52; Cosmopolitan of Las Vegas /José Andrés: 56; Scott Frances: 58, 70, 104; Kabuto: 60; Kaiseki Yuzu: 62; Khoury's: 64, 136; MGM Resorts International: 66; Penny Chutima: 72; Clint Jenkins: 74, 118; Venetian Resorts Las Vegas: 78; Bellagio/Michael Mina: 80; Boken Beauty Media/Nathan Rawlins: 82; Venetian/Palazzo: 84; Oh La La French Bistro/Richard Terzaghi: 86; Angela Ortaliza: 88, 157, 205; Pamplona: 92, 126; Naomi Mauro: 96; Raku & Sweets Raku: 98; Caesars Palace: 100; Sonia El-Nawal/Rooster Boy Café: 102; Bellagio: 106; Deke Castleman: 110; The Black Sheep: 112; The Kitchen at Atomic: 114; Twist: 116; Sasi Phothidokmai: 120; Wynn Las Vegas/Barbara Kraft: 122; Yui Edomae: 124; Christian Andrade: 128; Anthony Curtis: 129, 162, 165; Tanya Maynard: 130; Hatsumi: 134; Tatsujin X: 138; Chubby Cattle: 141; Tazeen: 145; 146; 148, 198, 201; Esther's Kitchen: 156; Vesta Coffee Roasters: 159; Palms/Scotch80 Prime: 160; SLS Las Vegas (Sahara)/Bazaar Meat: 163; Hannah Rushton: 168; Rosallie Le French Café: 169; Carlos Larios: 174; Gen3 Hospitality Group: 176; John Arena: 178; Pinkbox Doughnuts: 180; Locale Restaurant: 182; Grimaldi's: 185; Jenna Fisher: 186; Naked Fish: 191; Alder & Birch: 192; Casa Don Juan: 193; Forte European Tapas: 194; Jennifer Hippler/Hitchin' Post Saloon: 199; Mt. Charleston Lodge/ Cynthia Shaffer: 200; Darrell Craig Harris: 202; Cipriani: 203; Peppermill Lounge: 208; TAO Group: 212; Andiamo Steakhouse/the D: 213; Al Powers: 214; STK Las Vegas: 215; Marine Nunez: 216; Charles Sicuso: 218; Barbara Kraft: 222; Las Vegas Convention Center: 224

Dedication

To my mother, Ruth Curtas, who has taught me
so much and continues to do so to this day.

To Alan Richman and John Mariani, who
first inspired me and then became my friends.

And finally, to my wife, Alexandra, who never
ceases to bring joy to my life and a sparkle to the table.

AIR TRUFFLES AT 'E' BY JOSÉ ANDRÉS

Contents

Section I—The 52 Essential

John Curtas

Section II—Additional Recommendations

Section III—Index and Maps

SALMON SALAD AT SPAGO

Author's Note

What does "essential" mean?

Does it mean "the best"? Yes, but it signifies something more. The best will always be essential, but what is essential might not always be the best. When it comes to the restaurants of Las Vegas, "essential" stands for those that stand out and set a standard, the first places I'd take a visiting gourmet or a fellow food writer, the ones doing the most intriguing work in the kitchen, to which my mind always wanders when I'm hungry. They tend to be projects of passion, not money, eateries reflecting the particular sensibilities of their chefs and owners, not the calculations of a casino corporation. When I list a restaurant as "essential," it means I would take you there, my friend, if you dialed me up and asked, "John, what's a place I *have to* go to in Vegas right now?"

This is the eighth edition of *Eating Las Vegas*. For 10 years, this little guidebook has consumed my summers, expanded my waistline, lightened my wallet, and kept me patrolling the streets of Sin City for the best places to eat. I like to brag that no one has ever "eaten Las Vegas" as much as I have. Besides looking for strokes wherever we can find them, even when they're self-applied, it's true.

In the beginning, I wanted to write a book called *The Restaurants of Las Vegas*. My fantasy (way back in 1995 when my food writing career began in earnest) was to publish a guide similar to the ones coming out of New York: gourmet tours-de-force by writers like Bryan Miller and Seymour Britchky that explored the culinary canyons of the Big Apple. If you will allow me another self-congratulatory morsel, I think I recognized before anyone that Las Vegas was destined to become a world-class restaurant city and it would need someone to lead a certain type of discriminating consumer through the green-felt jungle to oases of dining pleasure worth their time and money.

By the time the first edition of this book was launched in the fall of 2010, I'd put 15 years into covering the Vegas restaurant scene. A decade later, more calories have been consumed than I can count and the landscape has changed so much that those days feel like a gauzy dream. The early editions featured only a handful of local restaurants as "essential." This year, almost half the book celebrates off-Strip eateries.

Local dining options have expanded and improved so much recently that the world has taken notice of what we Las Vegans have known since the early aughts: Vegas hotels contain a wealth of kitchen talent—young folks itching to strut their stuff for residents, not just fill the bellies of distracted tourists. True, the Great Recession hastened this migration for many chefs. But as with wine, stressed vines make for better juice and the rigors of the economic downturn gave bloom to vibrant neighborhood dining cultures, especially downtown and in Chinatown, where cash-strapped Gen Xers and Millennials demanded a better supply of quality grub at affordable prices.

In some ways, it seems like 2020 should be the natural end to this obsession of mine. Where once I was the only voice in the wilderness beseeching people to patronize better restaurants, now the Web is crawling with opinions on where you should eat. I've become a dinosaur and I know it. Never again will Las Vegas see someone as foolish as me—compelled to eat everywhere and try everything, spend a mountain of his or her own cash to promote worthy restaurants, and sacrifice success in one career (law) for notoriety in a much less lucrative one. In essence, what I've always been is an unpaid press agent for the best restaurants of Las Vegas.

But don't feel sorry for me. I've been paid and paid well—in fabulous food, great friends, and wonderful experiences stretching back for half of my adult life. And you paid for this book. For that, and for all of this, I'm grateful.

John Curtas

Introduction

"In the lexicon of lip-smacking, an 'epicure' is fastidious in his choice and enjoyment of food, just a soupçon more expert than a 'gastronome'; a 'gourmet' is a connoisseur of the exotic, taste buds attuned to the calibrations of deliciousness, who savors the masterly techniques of great chefs; a 'gourmand' is a hearty bon vivant who enjoys food without truffles and flourishes; a 'glutton' overindulges greedily, the word rooted in the Latin for 'one who devours.'

"After eating, an epicure gives a thin smile of satisfaction; a gastronome, burping into his napkin, praises the food in a magazine; a gourmet, repressing his burp, criticizes the food in the same magazine; a gourmand belches happily and tells everybody where he ate."

—William Safire

In the beginning, you're an omnivore—a gourmand, if you will—eating everything in sight, building up a culinary catalogue in your head (and palate) of every taste, every flavor, every texture you encounter with every bite. At first, you don't even know you're doing it; you just want to devour everything and learn as much about it as you can. But after you've eaten everything from fish tacos in Cancun to bouillabaisse in Marseille, the quest for quintessence is all you seek, be it in a burrito, a burger, or a Béchamel.

Becoming an epicure is no easy task. It takes years—decades, really—of eating, reading, cooking, traveling, and tasting. Anyone who thinks you can become a gourmet simply by eating in restaurants is a fool. You can no more learn about food by eating in a lot of restaurants than you can learn about music by attending a lot of concerts. Great restaurant meals are the payoff for all your hard work, and the older you get, the more you want to maximize your enjoyment of them.

This 8th edition of *Eating Las Vegas* is the result of my 29 years of searching for excellence in the Las Vegas food scene. It's the culmination of more meals than I can count (consider 10 restaurant meals a week times 50 weeks a year times 25 years and you'll get the idea), more calories than I need, and more tiramisu than any man should eat in a lifetime. But I've loved every minute of it. Even the bad meals have taught me something, and the ethereal life-changing epiphanies I've had in Las Vegas restaurants—Paul Bartolotta's roasted wild turbot, green-sauce chicken at Chengdu Taste, every bite I've ever had at Restaurant Guy Savoy—I wouldn't trade for the world.

To be sure, much is lacking in our food scene—agriculture being first and foremost. Ours is a top-down industry, enabled solely by the marketing muscle of the casino industry. Make no mistake, there's nothing "organic" about our restaurants. If not for the revolution wrought 25 years ago by Wolfgang Puck, Steve Wynn, Sheldon Adelson, and others, Las Vegas would still be the home of cheap prime rib and mountains of (frozen) shrimp cocktails. This is one of the reasons we get routinely ignored by the James Beard Foundation, which reveres the suffering-for-their-art chefs and looks upon our eateries as bloated, overstuffed, food factories for the Branson, Missouri, crowd.

But this book isn't interested in the mouths of the bargain-hunter fanny-packers. It's interested in *you*, reading these words. Because if you care enough to get this far in this introduction, you clearly have a certain dedication to eating well. And eating the best food in Las Vegas is what this book is all about.

Yes, it's a guidebook, but of more limited scope than many. If you expect a comprehensive tour of Las Vegas restaurants, look elsewhere. If you want to know whether some obscure (usually terrible) Italian place in some third-rate hotel is worth your dining-out dollar, consult Yelp, Thrillist, TripAdvisor, or any number of websites devoted to crowd-sourced opinion.

This book is as far from crowd-sourced opinion as you can get. I've seen the crowd; I've listened to the crowd; I've even been (on occasion) friends with the crowd; and you, my friend, should know that the crowd is generally full of beans when it comes to judging the best of the best. The crowd hasn't eaten in a restaurant every year

John Curtas

for a decade to see how it evolves; the crowd hasn't observed subtle changes from chef to chef; the crowd can't tell when that baguette is 30 minutes past its peak condition or that gelato has been kept at a few degrees south of perfect refrigeration. The public, God bless them, is concerned about bang for the buck. Yours truly, you need to know, doesn't give a fuck about bang for the buck.

No, all I care about is quality, quintessence, perfection—be it in a haunch of beef or a bunch of broccoli. Price isn't disregarded altogether, but comparing buffets isn't my interest or mission statement. (I leave that to the *Las Vegas Advisor* in the back of the book.) Telling you whether to drop a house payment at Joël Robuchon or a car payment at Bazaar Meat is what this tome is all about. If you're looking for the best Szechuan food in Chinatown, you've come to the right place. Best burgers in town? Step right in. If quintessential (expensive) Japanese floats your boat, we're here to help. On the other hand, if AYCE sushi is what you're after, you have my sympathies.

First and foremost, this book is a distillation of my never-ending quest for the best of Las Vegas. These are the best restaurants I've visited over the past year—the ones doing the most finely tuned cooking with the most unimpeachable ingredients. We've kept the "52 Essential" number in order to give you a workable framework to operate within. We've added a "Close, but No Cigar" section to recognize the many noteworthy places that may no longer merit an urgent visit, but are still worth a trip. And of course, the back of the book lists several hundred places, ranging from notable noodle parlors to terrific tacos—every one of them visited by me.

I'm proud to share my gustatory research with you, just as I'm proud to have covered this town so thoroughly and obsessively over the past three decades. Las Vegas is now one of the world's greatest restaurant cities—both on and off the Strip—and this book will guide you to the places that make it so. So grab a fork (or a pair of chopsticks) and dive in!

The Pros and Cons of Las Vegas Restaurants

Let's review the pros and cons of eating Las Vegas, to both inspire and warn you about what's really going on around here.

<u>Pros</u>

Fabulous French—As mentioned above, most American cities, outside of New York, are lucky to have one or two good French restaurants. We have 10.

Great steaks—Boffo beef abounds in our burg.

Incredible Italian—There are very good Italian restaurants in Vegas (Rao's, Carbone, Allegro, La Strega, and Locale) that didn't make the cut in this book.

Terrific Thai—Even our mediocre Thai restaurants, dozens of them, are pretty good. The top in town—Lotus of Siam—sports world-class wine program on par with its incendiary cooking.

Amazing Chinatown—Cheap and tasty eats abound only a mile west of the Strip. Leave your timidity behind and you'll have a feast for four for the price of a couple of cocktails at the Wynn/Encore.

Everyone's turning Japanese—In the past decade, righteous ramen, pullulating udon, exciting Edomae sushi, and great gyoza have invaded Chinatown. Be advised: The best stuff is in the 'burbs. Big-box Japanese, such as Nobu, Hakkasan, and Morimoto, are soooo 2010. The only people eating in them these days are vinyl-siding salesmen from Kansas.

Broad and deep wine lists—But at a price. See below.

Something for everyone—There are more good eats at the Aria Hotel than there are in any mid-sized city in America. And it's not the only hotel in Vegas that can make this claim.

Great service—Bad service on the Strip is almost non-existent.

Easy access—Make a reservation or just show up; someone will bust his or her ass to find you a seat.

No attitude—You won't find "mission statements" or "bad-boy-doing-it-his-way" chefs in Las Vegas.

Understandable food—See above.

Comfort—Strip restaurants never contracted the tiny-tables shitty-chairs virus that infects most hipster haunts in say, Seattle, D.C., or Brooklyn. The chairs are padded and the air conditioning always works.

John Curtas

Adult noise levels—A few joints around town are ear-splitting at prime times, but for the most part, you can hear yourself think while you're eating.

Great cocktails—Ever since the cocktail revolution took hold about a decade ago, it's been hard to get a bad drink in a Vegas hotel. Or even off the Strip, for that matter.

Top-shelf ingredients—Our best restaurants get meat, fish, and veggies on par with anyone's. True, 99% of it flies or drives to get here, but Chicago chefs don't exactly have fish jumping out of the ocean and onto their stoves either. Those vaunted New York sushi bars charging an arm and a leg for their omakase are getting the same fish, from the same Tokyo purveyors, as Yui and Kabuto are. And the bounty of California is a lot closer to us than it is to Atlanta.

People-watching—If you don't love people-watching in Vegas, you're either vision-impaired or not paying attention.

Sweet release—The pastry talent in Vegas is legendary. I'll stack the desserts coming out of our finest restaurants up against any, anywhere, anytime.

Cons

No imagination—If you're looking for highly personalized chef-driven food, look elsewhere, or off the Strip. With a few notable exceptions (our fabulous frog ponds being first and foremost), Vegas restaurants are food factories pure and simple. More than one chef has had his ambitions and enthusiasm crushed under the weight of feeding 500 picky eaters a day.

Overpriced wine—Las Vegas wine lists are best approached with a soothsayer, accountant, mortgage banker, and defibrillator on hand. A jar of K-Y jelly helps too. You'll also pay extra for that reach-around.

Overpriced drinks—The Strip is home to the $15 cocktail … which is fast becoming the $20 cocktail.

Incredibly bad Italian—Las Vegas is home to more terrible Italian restaurants than any city in the country. Amerigo Vespucci must roll over in his grave every night thinking of the slop being served in the name of his homeland in the land that he named.

Corporate soul-crushing sameness—Every goddamn restaurant in every goddamn hotel serves a pizza, and a pasta, and a salmon, and a chicken, and a steak, and a (bad) Caesar salad. Throw in a couple of trendy items like sliders, kale, bone marrow, and pork belly and you have your instant, interchangeable, eating experience! Reading Las Vegas menus is like living in an endless loop of a Guy Fieri fever dream.

Hoi polloi—Cargo shorts (men) and yoga pants (women) are everywhere. Usually on people with asses too big to be wearing them. Speaking of asses …

Dullards with money—Las Vegas is not, I repeat, not a gambling town; it's a convention town. Real gamblers throw money around like it's confetti; asshole conventioneers are livin' large for 3.5 days on the corporate credit card. Gamblers know how to behave in public; Middle Manager Mike from Milwaukee acts like he's never seen cleavage or a cote de boeuf before. Which he probably hasn't.

Celebrity chefs—I'm of two minds about celebrity chefs. On the one hand, our amazing restaurant scene wouldn't exist without them. If not for the corporate-branding ambitions of José Andrés, Wolfgang Puck, Michael Mina, et al., we'd still be living in prime rib purgatory. Twenty-five years ago, they saw gold in them thar hills and saved me from a life of "gourmet rooms," Continental cuisine, and coffee shops. On the other hand, many of them (not the four mentioned above) use Vegas like a late-night booty call for cash. Don't fool yourself: The only reason Giada, Morimoto, Gordon Ramsay, Bobby Flay, or Alain Ducasse show up twice a year is because they're contractually obligated to. The restaurants themselves are owned and run by the hotels.

Comps—Here's how comps work. You blow a lot of money gambling. The casino then gives you a voucher for something "free," usually a meal. You go to the restaurant to eat for "free." No money changes hands at the restaurant, but to ensure that you use up that comp as fast as possible, the restaurant (owned by or in cahoots with the hotel) charges insane markups. Everybody wins! Except those who pay with their own money and expect a fair exchange. I once saw a quartet of young Asian men stroll into a joint and sit down at a table with four bottles of Cristal champagne on each corner and a bowl of caviar the size of a basketball in the middle. They spent exactly ten minutes at the table, talked on their cell phones the whole time, and left without eating a thing. I paid $343 for my meal.

No one gives a shit about you; you're just a number—And when you leave, 10 more just like you are waiting for that seat. When you consider the numbers they do—a million a month in gross receipts is average—it's amazing how cordial Strip restaurants are. Most could act like carnival barkers when dealing with their ever-clamoring customers and still get away with it.

John Curtas

Food-and-beverage executives—There are exceptions but the "company-man" mentality that runs the F&B programs at most hotels is always threatening to turn Vegas into an armada of predictable franchised grub. Which works fine if you're a glorified accountant. Which most of them are.

Size matters—Most Vegas restaurants are behemoths. A 175-seat joint is average; places like Bazaar Meat seat more than 300. Intimate they're not. If you want intimacy, go to Le Cirque … or San Francisco.

Expense—Make no mistake: Vegas is the most expensive restaurant town in America. The mantra of the big hotels is "hit 'em hard, hit 'em fast, and wait for the next sucker to show up." The down-pricing and bargains instituted during the Great Recession are but a dim memory now. Sticker shock is everywhere; even the buffets will set you back a Benjamin (for two) these days. Big-city gourmands gasp when they see the cost of a prime steak or bottle of Cabernet out here. Personally, I go to other big cities (New York, L.A., Paris, Rome) when I want to dine well for less money. There's a lot of fantastic food in Las Vegas, but you'll pay through the nose for it.

Price Designations

At the top of each review is one of four price designations: $25 or less, $25-$75, $75-$125, or $125 and up. They provide a general guide to what it will cost you to dine there, based on the per-person price of an appetizer, an entrée, a side or dessert, and one or two lower-priced cocktails.

Who's In / Who's Out

Here's a quick list of the changes in the Essential 52 since the last edition of this book.

New in 2020

b.B.d.'s, China Mama, Cipriani, Hatsumi, Lamaii, Mabel's BBQ, Matteo's Ristorante Italiano, Mott 32, Oh La La French Bistro, Old Soul, Rooster Boy Café, Spago, Tatsujin X, The Black Sheep, The Kitchen at Atomic, Vetri Cucina, Weera Thai Kitchen

Gone from the Essential 52

Allegro, Andre's, Blue Ribbon, Boteco, Carbone, Chengdu Taste, Hiroyoshi, Japaneiro, Jean Georges Steakhouse, Julian Serrano, La Cave, Libertine Social, Morel's, Mr. Chow, Picasso, Prime, Trattoria Nakamura-Ya

CHILAQUILES AT ROOSTER BOY CAFE

Evolution of a Restaurant Critic

Food writer John Mariani once categorized three kinds of restaurant critics: "The slobs, the snobs, and the oh-goodie-goodies."

The slobs are professional writers who either get thrown into, or decide to write about, food sometime in mid-career. Being writers by trade, their qualifications for the gig (when they start out) usually consist of being able to write a cogent paragraph and knowing what they like to eat. Any editor will tell you a real writer who wants to become a food critic is preferable to a passionate foodie who wants to (try to) become a writer. Getting real writers to write about restaurants is usually a lot easier than getting them into a collared shirt.

Mariani properly pegged me as an "oh-goodie-goodie" type of critic years ago. For the longest time, I ate everything in sight and was pleased as punch that Las Vegas was taking its place on the world's gastronomic stage. Somewhere over the past decade, I shed my omnivorous obsessions and replaced them with unabashed epicurean snobbery, and therein lies the tale.

John Anthony Curtas was practically raised in American restaurants. As a preteen in the 1960s, I circumnavigated the United States with my family, eating in the best restaurants from Miami to Seattle, New York to New Orleans. My parents were hardly "to the menu born," but both had a healthy appreciation for good food and wanted their children (two sisters, a brother, and I) to experience the best of eating out. Neither parent was a gourmet; we never had wine or liquor in our house and seafood was as foreign to our table as chopsticks. But Mom and Dad loved going out to a restaurant—dressing us all up and making a night of it. To them, dining out was about the experience of leaving the confines of home and seeking the thrill of being served good food in a fabulous place where they waited on you hand and foot. Wherever we traveled, they always sought out the best restaurant in town and the best table in the house, the better to experience the theater of great dining.

As a young adult, I started cooking more out of poverty than choice. My older sister gave me a subscription to *Bon Appetit* magazine in 1978 that I ate up, literally and figuratively. An early girlfriend and the second Mrs. John A. Curtas were both foodies before such a term existed and they indulged my then-passion for Chinese food. By 1980, I'd pretty much cooked my way through *The Chinese Menu Cookbook* (Joanne Hush and Peter Wong, Holt Rinehart Winston, 1976) and was seduced by the Szechuan craze that was all the rage then. (Yes, there was a Szechuan craze in those prehistoric times and I have the cookbooks to prove it.)

My ex-wife was even so kind as to compile a list of Chinese grocery stores for me when we first moved to Vegas in 1981, so I could continue working my way through the various regional cuisines. Until around 1990, if you'd asked me what my favorite food in the world was, I would've answered the strong, salty, sour, and hot foods of the Szechuan and Hunan provinces of China. (Then and now, the textural nuances of Cantonese cooking and the folderol of Mandarin banquets remain more of a curiosity than a keen pursuit.)

Wedged into all of this was a move back east in the mid-1980s, where I lived a mere 50 miles from midtown Manhattan. It was a seminal time for American food and I consumed the New York restaurant scene wholesale, as Danny Meyer, Drew Nieporent, Larry Forgione, et al. developed a food-centric, wine-friendly, customer-casual template that put Baby Boomers at ease with sophistication without pretense.

In 1990, after five years of eating in places like Odeon, the Coach House, Four Seasons, Peter Luger, and the Union Square Café (not to mention enjoying the best seafood in America every summer on Nantucket), I moved back to Las Vegas and surveyed the edible landscape. It was not a pretty sight. The best restaurants in town were two chain steakhouses: Ruth's Chris and Morton's. Every hotel had five eateries: coffee shop, buffet, steakhouse, Italian, and a (not very) "gourmet room" serving "continental cuisine" from some unnamed continent. All of them faced the keno pit, or so it seemed. Marcel Taylor, the Caesars Palace dealer who brought Ruth's Chris to town in 1989, told me that the philosophy of every hotel back then was to capture casino customers and never let them out the front door. As he put it, "We had every place to eat right there. What more could the tourists want?"

But want they did, and when Ruth's Chris realized its Las Vegas outpost was outselling all its other franchises, the word quickly spread to upscale chains and chefs everywhere that Vegas was the place to be. Late 1992 brought the opening of Wolfgang Puck's Spago; soon thereafter Mark Miller, Charlie Trotter, and Emeril Lagasse planted their flags in the MGM. Suddenly, we had a real restaurant scene.

The only thing lacking was a serious critic to write about it. So I stepped into the breach. It took a year of hounding media outlets, but finally in October 1995, I got a shot at being the Nevada Public Radio food critic, a position I pretty much invented for myself and a gig that lasted until 2011. Did I know anything about radio? Absolutely not. But I knew a helluva lot about food, could put two sentences together, and looked great in a button-down shirt. As I like to say: In the land of the blind, the one-eyed man is king.

For five years, I was the only game in town when it came to critiquing serious restaurants in a serious way. It wasn't until 2001 that our main newspaper hired a full-time food writer and, in keeping with tradition, they made sure she was of the "My friend Edna had the steak and she thought it was a little chewy" school of food writing.

The '90s brought multiple trips to France and Italy and writing for all sorts of magazines and guidebooks. That was when I honed my palate and my writing. It took a decade-plus, but only after all those meals, reviews, and plane rides did I begin to appreciate my subject matter and my relationship to it.

Food is the most intimate relationship we will ever have and allowing strangers to cook it for us is an oddly perverse ritual that many struggle to understand. (It's the reason so many people have a chip on their shoulder when they eat out.) Giving over our bodies, our health, and our mouths to persons unknown and paying them for the privilege of feeding all three is surrendering an inordinate amount of power to a stranger. This curious dynamic continues to fascinate me as much as anything that I shove in my piehole.

As for the food, then and now the ingredient-driven Italians and technique-driven French have always intrigued my palate. French food—more than any other on Earth—is impelled by the extraction, concentration, and layering of flavors. Italian cuisine, in all of its regional glories, celebrates the simplicity of the raw material, while French cuisine tries to make it taste even more like itself. The yin and yang of these philosophies still hold me in their thrall and, of course, the French and Italians both make the best wine on the planet (sorry Spain and California).

Enter Japan. Japanese food is about the quest for perfection and in many ways, eating Japanese food in the U.S. and Japan has refined my tastes even further and eliminated my helter-skelter insatiability. No longer am I a galloping gourmand, happily ingesting everything in sight. Now in my sixties, I seek the unobtainable grail of the quintessential. Like a Japanese chef, I take interest in the details of the divine. A wasted meal, or even an ingredient, puts me in a bad mood. I've eaten so much of everything that I now simply want the best of anything, be it in a street taco, a glass of wine, or a piece of fish.

I'm no longer an "oh-goodie-goodie" and I'm certainly not a slob. It's said that to become a gourmet, like becoming a first-class horseman, you have to start young. I'm an epicure and I did start very young. But many more steps are ahead of me and it's this mountain that I continue to climb.

John Curtas

Twenty Suggestions for Dining Out in Style

1. Be in a good mood. You'll get out of restaurants what you put into them. If you're looking for a slight, or a service misstep, or a flabby French fry, you'll find it. The happier you are with yourself, the less small glitches will bother you.

2. Be hungry. A surprising number of people who go out to eat aren't hungry.

3. Be in love with restaurants. What's not to love? A number of people (usually young, always attractive) are scurrying around trying to feed you and please you. A surprising number of people who go out to eat don't want to be there. Restaurants are like relationships: You must really want to be in one to make it work.

4. If you want great service in a restaurant, go there several times in a relatively short period of time. Time #1 will be pleasant enough, time #2 they'll be happy to see you again, and by time #3, you'll be treated like one of the family. When you start getting treated like one of the family, some freebie (a drink, a dessert, a taste of something special from the kitchen) usually starts showing up. By trip #3, you will also look like a total stud to whomever you're dining with.

5. Be open-minded. Restaurants aren't for picky eaters. Picky eaters should prepare their own meals at home.

6. Remember how hard it is to own or work at a restaurant. Nothing is as easy as it seems. A cook is remembering a dozen details; the dishwasher is up to his elbows in 200-degree steam; the pretty little hostess is tracking who's coming and going while she's answering the phone, seating people, and trying to keep the owner's hand off her ass.

7. Respect the staff. Be grateful they're serving you and not the other way around.

8. Look at the menu carefully. Every restaurant in the world tells

you right up front what it's good at. If there's a box at the top or bottom of the page that says: "Try our world-famous waffles!" get the friggin' waffles. *Don't* get the lasagna, fer chrissakes. If you insist on ordering a cheeseburger at place advertising wood-fired pizzas, don't say I didn't warn you.

9. Listen to the staff. Ask them what they like. Be honest with them when they ask you questions.

10. Don't ask too many questions. You're there to eat; the waiters are there to bring you food, not discuss breakthroughs in animal husbandry or the pedigree of the vegetables.

11. Be decisive. No one likes to watch you fret over the linguine versus the ravioli. Being too choosy in good restaurants is a bit like being finicky about oral sex: No matter what, you'll still enjoy yourself.

12. Only order fish in restaurants specializing in fish.

13. Order champagne right off the bat. Admittedly, this is one of my pricier pieces of advice, but if you order two glasses of expensive French champagne (or better yet, a bottle of the pricey stuff) as soon as you sit down, the wait staff will snap to your attention immediately. Works every time.

14. Unless you enjoy polluting your body with the refuse of the land and sea, avoid all-you-can-eat anything.

15. Leave your food allergies at home. Face it: You're not really allergic to anything; you just want the attention or you're fat. Or both.

16. Never order a glass of wine in cocktail bar. Never order a cocktail in a wine bar. Why do I have to keep telling you these things?

17. Show your enthusiasm. I don't care if you're in an izakaya in Tokyo, a Michelin-starred haute cuisine palace in Paris, or a lunch counter in Paducah, Kentucky, tell your waiter how happy you are to be there.

18. Dress the fuck up. If you look like a slob, you'll be treated like a slob. (Exception: barbecue restaurants. No one gives a shit how you look in a barbecue restaurant. Barbecue restaurants are the great equalizers.)

19. Never eat out on a Saturday night. Saturday night is to eating out what New Year's Eve is to drinking. Epicureans eat out on Wednesday and Thursday, when both the food and the staff are the freshest.

20. "Never eat at a place called Mom's, play cards with a man named Doc, or sleep with a woman whose troubles are worse than your own." — Nelson Algren

John Curtas

The Glories of Dining Alone

The Roman general Lucius Lucinius Lucullus Ponticus was one of the richest men in ancient Rome. He was known for his sumptuous banquets and feasts so elaborate (for dozens and sometimes hundreds of guests) that Pompey and Cicero refused an invitation to dine with him, fearing for the expense he'd incur for even a simple dinner.

A famous story tells of Lucullus taking his chief cook to task for a modest repast placed before the general as he dined alone. "As there were to be no guests, I thought my master would not want an expensive supper," said his chef by way of an apology.

"What?" exclaimed Lucullus. *"Dost thou not know that this evening, Lucullus dines with Lucullus?"*

If you're one of those who dreads, avoids, or maybe just hasn't mastered the art of dining alone, you're truly missing something special. Eating alone, especially in a good restaurant, is one of life's great pleasures.

I didn't always feel this way, of course. Like many of you, I used to be embarrassed to sit alone in a crowded eatery, feeling pathetic and stared-at the whole time. Rushing through the meal, I savored little and cringed a lot at my sad lonely life.

But then I saw the light.

When you make the decision (or the decision is made for you) to dine alone, look at the freedom and the unbridled hedonism that lie before you. When you dine alone:

- You can order what you want, when you want.
- There's no menu bartering with your dining companions. ("If you're having the pompano, and she's taking the salmon, I guess I'll have the sole, just for the halibut.")

- You can get as stewed as you want (as long as you're not driving).
- Table manners? Why bother?
- You can fill up on bread, or, even better, scarf down butter or olive oil with impunity. I'll admit that I enjoy shamelessly dipping a host of breads into the butter with no regard for knife or dish. Barbaric? Well, yes, but oh so satisfying.
- Red wine with fish? No problem. Three gimlets before the degustation? Why not?
- Eating salsa is so much easier. We all know how everyone has to finesse dipped chips into their mouths, avoiding the dreaded double-dip. Well, shoveling your salsa solo eliminates all that, and you don't have to share.
- You can flirt shamelessly with the hot hostesses, waitresses, or waiters, depending on who's floating your boat that evening.
- You can eat with your fingers, mix up stuff on various plates— even drink up the sauce.
- On a more serious note, you save money. The cost of a meal at gourmet destinations like Le Cirque, Savoy, or Robuchon is prohibitive. Go alone and you can concentrate on the food, discussing it in depth with the highly knowledgeable wait staffs (at least those you're not trying to pick up). Chatting up the staff becomes an education and a way to make a new friend, at a pittance of the price if two or more are present.

So, the next time you truly want to luxuriate in a great meal, try remembering that the word "luxurious" comes from the name of the noble Roman—who had no greater dining companion than when he, Lucullus, dined with himself.

John Curtas

The Future of Las Vegas Dining

I've been lucky.

I've had a front-row seat for the biggest restaurant revolution any American city has ever seen.

What began as a third-rate town slinging second-rate food has become one of the world's greatest dining cities. But what made Las Vegas famous will not be what keeps us there. The issue confronting us now is: What's next for our restaurant scenes on and off the Strip?

My good fortune has probably given me as clear a crystal ball as anyone's, and for the next decade, I foresee the slow retreat of celebrity chefs, the rise of the Asian gastro-tourist, and the continued expansion of our local chef-driven restaurant culture.

We're two decades removed from the celebrity-chef boom that put Las Vegas on the world's gastronomic map. Very few name chefs "move the needle" any longer the way Wolfgang Puck, Emeril Lagasse, and Mario Batali once did. Gordon Ramsay's marketing muscle comes from being on TV 24/7, but that won't last forever, and there will be no afterlife in re-runs. Giada de Laurentiis may appeal to Midwestern housewives, but cooking shows like hers are passé and Millennials don't flock to her brand of sunny aspirational perfection, with windblown hair and copious cleavage anointing the manicotti. The names that made Las Vegas restaurants great—Maccioni, Vongerichten, Flay, Nobu, Mina, et al.—don't have the caché they once did, and only José Andrés seems to have cultivated a younger following to match his outsized personality. Who will replace them? That question keeps casino executives awake at night.

My prediction is it will be "name chefs" with a different sort of celebrity than the pioneers and big stars of the early aughts. The Food Network made household names out of Guy Fieri, Cat Cora, and Bobby Flay, but to be blunt, none of them was respected for their kitchen talents. There is only so much gochujang David Chang can sling and Michael Symon, God bless him, is no Wolfgang Puck. Fieri is likeable enough, but even he knows how terrible his restaurants are. Most of them wanted to become television stars and that's what they did. But in the 21st century, a TV chef confers about as much credibility as being the White House press secretary. The next generation wants quality and integrity on the plate, not sell-outs pretending to be chefs so they can cash in on fame.

The new generation is seeking chefs like Marc Vetri and restaurants like Matteo's (formerly The Factory Kitchen), highly respected operators who bring serious foodie cred to their outlets. The restaurants that come here in the next decade will have established reputations, but their credibility, be they a barbecue joint in Austin or a haute-cuisine palace from San Francisco, will be based on a certain gravitas they've established with the food cognoscenti … whether those in the know are actual epicures or the Instagram crowd.

In that vein, it will be interesting to see how the nouveau Latino Cosme performs at the Wynn when it arrives in late 2019. Mexico City's Enrique Olvera is one of the world's elite chefs and his New York outpost, Cosme, has been a hit in New York since its opening. But the average Vegas visitor doesn't know Enrique Olvera from Pancho Villa. The difference today versus 20 (or even 10) years ago is that within seconds, in the palm of their hand, those same out-of-towners can find out just what a big deal he is in New York and Mexico. If he succeeds and if deluxe chains like Cipriani and Mott 32 make their mark here, you can expect to see more of the same, from upscale American restaurateurs (Stephen Starr? Danny Meyer, perhaps?) to Asia (Tim Ho Wan opened at the Palms as this book went to the printer).

Tim Ho Wan provides the perfect example of my second prediction: a full-blown Asian invasion—in particular, an influx of well-funded Asian restaurants (hello, Mott 32!) from California, China, and Korea whose principals see Las Vegas as fertile ground for siphoning dining-out dollars from pan-Pacific travelers sure to be the next big demographic. Let's face it, Baby Boomers are dying out, their kids don't like to gamble, and the burgeoning middle class of China is just itching to come here. They bring numbers, cash, and a love of gambling guaranteed to water the inside of any casino owner's mouth. And they all need to eat.

Thus, in the future, every hotel-casino will boast more and better Asian restaurants, almost all of them imports—names that don't mean a thing to you and me, but that signal a certain level of comfort to their clientele as surely as a Cheesecake Factory appeals to a soccer mom. This subtle infiltration has already started on Spring Mountain Road. A couple of years ago, suddenly three slick well-financed Korean barbecue joints popped up. The new Shanghai Plaza has a dozen new eateries, many of them from southern California or Seoul. Mom and pops they're not and they foreshadow a time when the low-key charm of Chinatown gives way to savvy investors throwing big money our way and driving up real estate prices. This isn't a future prediction, it's already happening.

For the time being, though, Chinatown and downtown are where the action is—where to find our most organic from-the-ground-up restaurants and where the food is best. What began five years ago with Carson Kitchen has begat a wellspring of kitchen talent, from Dan Krohmer and Vincent Rotolo to James Trees, moving away from the Strip because they want to be part of a community, not just a functionary in a giant food factory.

Off the Strip will still be a struggle for small operators. Like most of the West, Vegas long ago sold its soul to large real estate developers, ensuring that the relentless mediocrity of national franchises will continue to dominate our landscape. And they will continue to do so until the public wises up to the fact that these chains are slowly killing us with their pre-processed consistency.

But unlike when I started this gig a quarter-century ago, today a ready supply of cooks and customers want to find each other. In doing so, they've raised the quality of dining throughout the Vegas valley. For this, all epicures, gastronomes, gourmands, and gourmets (or just folks who like a good plate of grub) should be grateful. Opening a restaurant based on passion will always be a crapshoot facing long odds, but it's a blessing that in Las Vegas, in the 21st century, so many talented chefs will continue to roll the dice.

DEVIL'S EGGS AT CARSON KITCHEN

Section I

The 52 Essential

BARDOT BRASSERIE

French

Aria at CityCenter
1-877-230-2742
aria.com
Mon.-Fri., 5:30-10:30 p.m.; Sat. & Sun., 9:30 a.m.-10:30 p.m.
$25-$75

When Michael Mina announced he was closing American Fish at Aria and replacing it with a classic French brasserie, more than a few foodies scoffed. Didn't he know that this is the age of tiny tables, minuscule plates, insulting noise levels, and uncomfortable everything? Hadn't someone told him that traditional French style is about as hip as a dickey? And that Croque Madame and salad Niçoise were old hat by the Clinton era?

They might have told him, but we're happy he didn't listen. Instead, what he did was bring forth a drop-dead-delicious ode to the golden era of brass, glass, and béchamel-drenched sandwiches—hearty platters of wine-friendly food that many think went out of style with tasseled menus, but didn't. It just took a break for a decade.

With BB, the reasons all of these recipes became famous to begin with has come roaring back, to the delight of diners who want to be coddled and cosseted with cuisine, not challenged and annoyed. Mina had the prescience to know this, and the good sense to hire Executive Chef Josh Smith to execute his vision. Smith is an Ameri-

John Curtas

can through and through, but obviously has a deep feeling for this food, and every night (and via the best weekend brunch in town), he proves why classics never go out of style and overwrought, over-thought, multi-course tasting menus may soon go the way of the supercilious sommelier.

Make no mistake, Bardot Brasserie is a throwback restaurant, but a throwback that captures the heart and soul of real French food like none of its competition. It harkens to an age of comfort food from a country that pretty much invented the term. What sets it apart is the attention to detail. Classics like steak frites and quiche are cli-chés to be sure, but here they're done with such aplomb, you'll feel like you're on the Left Bank of Paris, only with better beef. The pâté de campagne (country house-made pâté) is a wondrous evocation of pressed pork of the richest kind, and the escargots in puff pastry show how a modern chef can update a classic without sacrificing the soul of the original recipe. The skate wing suffers not at all from being 6,000 miles from the Champs Elysée, and the lobster Thermi-dor—bathed in Béarnaise and brandy cream—is a glorious testa-ment to the cuisine of Escoffier.

Most of all, though, Bardot Brasserie is an homage to the great homey restaurants of France. By going old school, Michael Mina has set a new standard in Franco-American style and made me realize what I was missing all along.

GET THIS

Lobster Thermidor; skate wing; Croque Madame; onion soup grantinée; foie gras parfait; steak tartare; duck wings à l'Orange; king crab crêpe; seared foie gras Lyonnaise; frisée aux lardons; sole meu-niere; chicken roti; oak-smoked Duroc pork chop; brunch.

BAZAAR MEAT BY JOSE ANDRES (STRIP) Steakhouse

Sahara Las Vegas
(702) 761-7610
saharalasvegas.com
Sun.-Thurs., 5:30-10 p.m.; Fri. & Sat., 5:30-11 p.m.
$75-$125

José Andrés is a high priest of meat and this is his temple. Calling it a steakhouse, however, is a bit unfair, since the seafood and wacky Spanish creations (molecular olives, cotton-candy foie-gras foam, etc.) are every bit as good as the steaks. For pure carnivorous joy, I'll put Bazaar up against any porterhouse pit in the country, any day, but I'll also stake its tapas and sausage and gutsy Spanish comfort food against any this side of the Iberian Peninsula.

There's a raw bar, a ham bar, a real bar, and a bar-none selection of steaks. With all of this in mind, you will, of course, not want to miss the roasted suckling pig or the whole roasted wild turbot. That little piggy can be ordered whole in advance for a crowd of 8-10; quarter portions are available on short notice (although not usually on the menu) for smaller tables.

And if all that's not enough to distract you, the wine list may be the best Spanish card in the country.

Before you get to the big proteins, though, you'll have to navigate side one of the blackboard-sized menu. There, you'll find all sorts of temptations that will fill you up long before Porky's left leg

John Curtas

appears. Lighter appetites should stick with fresh raw scallops, gazpacho shots, and José's Asian taco (ham, nori, topped with flying fish roe), while heartier souls will want to dive into the croquetas (stuffed with creamy ham or chicken) or the Reuben, a hollowed-out crispy mini-football of air bread upon which pastrami is draped. The super-giant light-as-a-saltine chicharron takes up half the table, but disappears quickly as it's dipped in Greek yogurt with za'tar spices, and everyone will be fighting over the last bite of patatas bravas.

One of the signs of a great steakhouse is how they treat their veggies and here, if you don't want to think about meat (difficult under the circumstances, but doable), you can splurge on stuffed piquillo peppers, Catalan spinach with raisins and pine nuts, Brussels sprouts petals with lemon purée, or a whole cauliflower steak with preserved lemon. The beefsteak tomato tartare gets the most oohs and aahs (looking like the brightest red small pizza you've ever seen), but the simple tomato salad and the endive Caesar are show-stoppers as well.

If you haven't gotten the idea by now, this is a huge menu, both sides of that big plastic board, in fact, and deciding what to eat can be somewhat daunting. The good news is they pull everything off, nightly, with the precision of a Marine Corps drill team.

When you finally get to the steaks, you'll find all the usual suspects: grain-fed, grass-fed, sirloined, flat-ironed, and skirted, but the thing to get is the "vaca vieja" eight- to ten-year-old rib steak—beef from old cows being the current fad among serious meat mavens. Aged on the hoof rather than in a locker, it competes with the best of dry-aged steaks for pure beefy minerality.

Like I said, calling this place a steakhouse is a bit of a misnomer. It's a palace of protein that even a pescatarian or a vegetarian can love. It's also one of the greatest restaurants in the world.

GET THIS

Cotton-candy foie gras; pork-skin chicharron; José's Asian taco; croquetas; Ferran Adria olives; patatas bravas; Reuben sandwich; tomato tartare; beef tartare; oysters; clams; live scallops; chef's selection of cured meats; piquillo peppers; Brussels sprouts petals; cauliflower steak; endive Caesar salad; tortilla sacromonte egg omelet with sweetbreads; grilled Galician-style octopus; roast suckling pig; whole roasted turbot; Wagyu beef cheeks; flat-iron steak; "vaca vieja" rib steak.

B.B.D.'S (WEST)

Palace Station
(702) 221-6513
palacestation.sclv.com
Mon.-Fri., 4:30-10 p.m.; Sat.-Sun., 11 a.m.-10 p.m.
$25 or less

In late 2018, this 300-seat meat emporium quietly opened in the refurbished Palace Station, bringing forth a gargantuan menu of everything from burgers and dry-aged steaks to bowls of duck ramen and hot chicken to never-seen-before dishes like Buffalo burnt chicken wings, Japanese duck drumsticks, and kimchi fries. It also poured the best (not the biggest) beer selection in town. So much was so good so fast about b.B.d.'s, it was a shock to the Vegas culinary ecosystem—and in the original locals casino to boot.

b.B.d.'s stands for burgers, Beers, and desserts, but that's only half the story. It's also a sports bar, a casual steakhouse, and a vegan restaurant. You'll find enhanced versions of Philadelphia's best sandwiches, along with Bavarian pretzels, lamb gyros, house-cured pastrami, housemade hot dogs, and house-aged beef, making this the all-star utility infielder of Vegas meateries.

They offer 20 (!) different sauces (all made in-house), potatoes a number of ways (the classic French fries are potato perfection), three salads (if you insist), and the usual frivolous fat-filled fried stuff (onion rings, poppers, cheese sticks, and such). But your attention is drawn to the meat from the moment you walk past the butcher

John Curtas

shop at the entrance and the real stars of the show are the burgers made with in-house-ground beef; they're juicy and packed with the kind of dense mineral-rich beefiness that's but a wisp of memory in the hamburgers most people consume. The beef here tastes like it could've come straight from Delmonico or CUT. The grind is coarse and the packing is just firm enough to hold together and sear properly, the better to retain the juiciness essential for burger apotheosis.

Three are offered. The 12-ounce dry-aged prime steakhouse burger is aged for 40-50 days and achieves that tinge of gaminess true beef aficionados look for.

The griddle burger elevates the In-N-Out template; one bite and you might forswear In-N-Out forever. And the steamed burger mimics the chopped-onion gray-meat magnificence of a White Castle slider. It tastes like White Castles that are three times thicker, sandwiched in a superior bun, and doesn't lie in your gut like a greasy brick. (Not that there's anything wrong with that, especially if you've been parkin g booze there all night.) Put them all together and you have a hamburger hamlet of unbridled greatness, the likes of which Vegas has never seen under one roof.

I'd be remiss if I didn't tout the steaks here too. They do a complete lineup from miso skirt to Flintstonian tomahawk, each the equal of beef a mile to the east at slightly softer prices.

If you have room and even if you don't, don't miss dessert: Gooey Warm Cinnabomb, wood-fired s'mores, waffle bread pudding, and liquid chocolate cake. Each is over the top and feeds at least two.

All of this is the handiwork of one Ralph Perrazzo, a Long Island chef (and Bradley Ogden alum) who won some TV burger battle, paving the way for his expansion to Vegas. I don't take those contrived competitions seriously anymore, but Perrazzo's meat mastery cannot be denied. His burgers are the best in Las Vegas.

GET THIS

Bavarian pretzel; mac & cheese; pickle fries; Korean BBQ fries; lamb gyro; duck/vegetable ramen; hot chicken sandwich; My Cousin Philly cheesesteak; Philadelphia's Other Brother roast pork sandwich; spicy Buffalo burnt wings; Japanese duck drumsticks; hot pastrami sandwich; house-made hot dogs; prime steakhouse burger; griddle burger; steamed mini-burgers; tomahawk steak; miso skirt steak; porterhouse; s'mores; Cinnabomb; liquid chocolate cake; and beer. Don't forget the beer.

Venetian
(702) 414-6200
venetian.com
5-10 p.m., daily; Mon.-Thurs., 7 a.m.-1 p.m.; Fri.-Sat., 7 a.m.-2 p.m.;
Oyster bar: Fri.-Sun., 3-10 p.m.
$75-$125

Thomas Keller took some pretty big hits last year. Per Se's demotion to two stars in the *New York Times* had the Internet (and *schadenfreude*-obsessed food press) all atwitter about his possibly losing his fastball. He might not be the pitcher he once was back there in Yankee Stadium, but out here in the hustings, his control is as pinpoint as ever. The epi baguettes can still blow you away from the first bite and they, like everything else on this menu, are major league. You won't find better oysters or mussels this far from an ocean and the room is just as vibrant and comfortable as it was when it opened 13 years ago.

I've eaten here dozens of times over those years and the food—whether a special silken corn soup or voluptuous veal porterhouse—never fails to astonish with its technical perfection and intensity. The wine list, like most in Gouge the Greenhorn Gulch, sticks it to you without lubrication. On the bright side, there's a nice selection of half bottles that bend you over for half the insanely inflated price. Stick with whites and light reds (think Beaujolais and vin du pays) to avoid feeling quite so violated. Those quibbles aside, asking me to choose between Bouchon and Bardot Brasserie for casual French supremacy is like asking me which one of my kids I love the most.

GET THIS

Oysters; soupe a l'oignon; corn soup (seasonal); steak frites; parfait du foie gras; moules au safran; poulet roti; truite amandine; Croque Madame; escargot; salade Lyonnaise; veal chop; boudin blanc; crème brûlée; bouchons.

CARSON KITCHEN (DOWNTOWN) American

see map 1, page 233
124 S. Sixth Street
(702) 473-9523
carsonkitchen.com
Sun.-Wed., 11:30 a.m.-10 p.m.; Thurs.-Sat., 11:30 a.m.-11 p.m.
$25-$75

Downtown Las Vegas continues to exhibit the schizophrenia of a town founded by Mormons that makes its living off drinking, gambling, and whoring. After 112 years, it still doesn't know whether it wants to be a collection of low-rent cheap-ass casinos or a place in which people might actually want to live and hang out. The nickel-beer crowd still flocks to that gawdawful awning over the old Fremont Street; younger hipper folks (who look at slot machines the way Brigham Young did monogamy) eschew the buskers, beggars, and bunco artists for the cooler confines (as in more au courant) of East Fremont and its surrounding blocks.

Meanwhile, there's almost nothing good to eat in the downtown hotels, but Carson Kitchen dishes up a great plate of grub, as well as some hope for the future. The only problem with CK is its size. Seating only 40, it fills up quickly. And when it's full, it's loud. Too loud for Boomers of a certain age, but just what Gen-Xers and Millennials seem to find appealing. Personally, I ignore the amplitude and concentrate on the amplifood. Because whatever you get will ring your chimes to go along with that ringing in your ears.

John Curtas

The menu is small but mighty and there's not a clunker on it. The communal "social plates" always get you started on the right foot: Crispy chicken skins come with smoked honey and gyro tacos get stuffed with lamb and tzatziki. They compete with barbecue burnt ends slathered in sauce and veal meatballs coated with sherry-foie gras cream. The bacon jam with baked brie is no slouch either and the sour-sweet artichoke is a thistle that will whet your whistle. A "filet-ohhh-fish" is more like a fishcake than a filet and comes with a green goddess cole slaw, the rotating cast of flatbreads are flat-out wonderful, and the "Secret Sunday Chicken" puts Chick-fil-A to shame. Sure, it costs twice as much, but it's also twice as good. The "Butter Burger," an homage to Wisconsin, is all you could want in an upscale patty and the short-rib grilled cheese (oozing with fromage) is … wait for it … gouda enough for two.

Bigger proteins, such as sea bass, strip steak, and chops, get treated with respect (and in-your-face sauces) and the "farm-and-garden" options are, simply stated, wonderful.

They rotate things seasonally here, but the baked mac and cheese is always present, as are the mega-rich black rice with oxtail risotto and the spicy shrimp and grits. In summer, don't miss the watermelon and feta, and whenever they're on the menu, close your eyes and order whatever this kitchen is doing with Brussels sprouts, broccoli, or cauliflower.

Simplicity is the secret to CK's success. If you eat there a lot, as I do, you notice the straightforward recipes and direct flavors. The reach of this kitchen never exceeds its grasp, even as it constantly stretches for excellence. In some ways, the food is like the room: boisterous and a little too small for its ambitions. Downtown denizens wouldn't have it any other way.

GET THIS

Crispy chicken skins; bacon jam with brie; tempura green beans; gyro tacos; veal meatballs; BBQ burnt ends; devil's eggs; grilled artichoke; butter burger; filet-ohhh-fish; secret Sunday chicken sandwich; pork chop; sea bass; flatbreads; shrimp & grits; watermelon and feta; black rice and oxtail risotto; bourbon fudge brownie; glazed-donut bread pudding.

CHINA MAMA (WEST)

Chinese

see map 1, page 233
3420 S. Jones Boulevard
(702) 873-1977
chinamamavegas.com
11 a.m.-10 p.m., daily
$25 or less

In much the same way that Lotus of Siam gave Vegas its first taste of authentic northern Thai (in 1999), China Mama brought a taste of Shanghai to our doorstep. Before it opened (2008), authentic Shanghainese soup dumplings (soup-filled pillows of ethereal porcine bliss known as xiao long bao) were unheard of, not to mention such delicacies as lamb with cumin, fish with pickled greens, and cubed pork buried under an avalanche of chiles. But the dumplings, whether steamed, fried, or filled with pork or shrimp, were all the rage as Vegas finally escaped the from behind the bars of its sweet-and-sour Chinese prison.

Then ownership changed, chefs moved on, and China Mama's food started a slow steady decline. Of course, if you asked management why things were different, they said with a straight face, "Everything same," but you knew it wasn't. Things got so bad that we wrote the place off altogether about four years ago and vowed never to return.

About a year ago, a woman named Ivy Ma took over the place, closed it down for some months, and restored China Mama to its

John Curtas

former glory. Ma opened up the kitchen and placed it behind a giant glass wall that proudly advertises the fresh Chinese buns that originally made this place famous. You can watch her cooks work their magic on packets of doughy deliciousness you won't find anywhere in Vegas this good for prices this reasonable.

Head straight to the pastry section of the menu, just like in the old days, for the steamed and pan-fried pork buns, as essential to a meal here as chopsticks and hot tea. The green-onion pancake, beef roll, and potstickers are also top-shelf, but to mistake this place as exclusively a dumpling palace would be doing it a great disservice. Crispy duck, jumbo shrimp, and dry pepper chicken hold their own with those dumplings, as does sliced fish with pickled mustard.

Other menu items ranging from the simple (cucumber salad with mashed garlic) to the sublime Awesome Meatball in Clay Pot are by turns gutsy and refined, all bursting with eastern Chinese pungency. Even the standard-issue stuff manages to sing: Szechuan tantan noodle and twice-cooked pork with spicy sauce are sinus-clearers and the sliced fish in hot chili sauce will never be accused of false advertising. The mapo tofu is exemplary and even the uninspiring-sounding sautéed Chinese lettuce comes draped in a velvety sauce that gets your attention.

The new menu is easy to navigate (the old one was a multi-page disaster of numbers and fractured prose) and even has pictures to entice the bold and assuage the timid. The servers are bilingual, informed about the menu, and attentive, a far cry from the perfunctory politeness usually dished out along Spring Mountain Road.

Resistance to the don tot (Portuguese egg tarts) for dessert is futile, so order them as soon as you sit down and you won't have to wait while they're freshly made. They come two to an order and one order is never enough. As for liquids, they bring you hot tea, but you have to ask for water. Just like in China.

GET THIS

Eight-piece steamed juicy pork buns; Mama's Special pan-fried pork buns; potstickers; Mama's crispy beef; dry pepper chicken; beef rolls; crispy layered pancake; pancake with scallion; sliced fish in hot chili sauce; sliced fish fillet with pickled mustard; sizzling beef in black pepper sauce; Awesome Meatball in Clay Pot; stir-fried lamb with cumin; twice-cooked pork; orange chicken; mapo tofu; sautéed Chinese lettuce; Szechuan tantan noodle; dot tot.

CIPRIANI (STRIP)   Italian

Wynn Las Vegas
(702) 777-7390
wynnlasvegas.com
11:30 a.m.-4 p.m., daily;
Dinner: Mon.-Thurs., 4-11 p.m.; Fri. & Sat., 4 p.m.-midnight
$25-$75

Cipriani is a different sort of Italian restaurant. The ease and grace with which it displays its good taste are something new—refinement and subtlety being to Las Vegas what strippers are to the Piazza San Marco. But there's a seductive reassuring quality to its atmosphere and flavors. Nothing overpowers, but each bite beckons another; every visit inspires a return. The cuisine is born of nuance and the service has been honed by almost a century of tradition.

Las Vegas is now home to the world's 19th Cipriani and it references the look of the original: Tables are low and the bold tan, white, and dark-blue color scheme bespeaks a slightly nautical unpretentious elegance. Those tables are always covered in starched white linens and the sleek and sexy décor—all polished woods and gleaming brass—makes everyone feel like they're in a Cary Grant movie.

Upon entering, you'll have a Bellini: a small glass of Prosecco and white-peach juice invented in the summer of 1948. After the Bellini, you'll have the carpaccio: the other world-famous invention of Giuseppe Cipriani.

The polenta, salt cod (baccala Mantecato), cuttlefish, veal with

John Curtas

tuna sauce, and calf's liver alla Veneziana don't spring to mind when most Americans think Italian food, but the recipes, straight from Venice, are as compelling as any carbonara and a lot easier on the waistline.

Baby artichokes alla Romana might be the best you've ever had. Pappa al pomodoro is an addictively sweet dense wad of tomato pulp, while salads of endive and radicchio, and lobster with avocado, will serve as palate cleansers before you lean into excellent prosciutto and thin slices of bresaola. Seafood lovers are equally well-served by the sweet-sour anchovies and the seppie in tecia, a thick black stew of cephalopod ink enveloping tender cuttlefish strands that's as far from fried calamari as foie gras is from chopped liver.

Pastas are where things get heftier. Portions easily feed two and it's doubtful you've ever had a veal ragú as light as the one dressing thick strands of tagliardi. You'll wonder if ham, peas, and cheese have ever matched better with tortellini or if a Parmesan cream sauce has ever baked more beautifully as a crust for thin eggy tagliolini, another signature dish. Knuckle-sized gnocchi come dressed with tomato cream one day, Gorgonzola the next, and are surprisingly light despite their weighty descriptions.

They do a beautiful Dover sole alla Mugnaia (a.k.a. meuniere) here, wonderful langoustines al forno, gorgeous veal al limone, and a rib-sticking braised short rib (again, all easily feed two), but if you really want to eat like the Doge of Venice, tuck into that sweet, sour, onion-laced calf's liver.

Pizza also makes an appearance and it's more than an afterthought. In fact, it's among the best on the Strip … even if pizza is about as Venetian as chicken chow mein.

Desserts are remarkably light and white: dolce vanilla meringue cake, a Napoleon with vanilla cream, vanilla panna cotta, and the thickest, creamiest, silkiest and most vanilla-y gelato you've ever tasted.

GET THIS

Bellini, carpaccio, bresaola, anchovies, lobster salad, octopus salad; minestrone; pizza, artichokes alla Romana; seppie in tecia (cuttlefish stew); baccala Mantecato (salt cod); anything with polenta; tagliardi with veal ragú; ham and pea tortellini; baked tagliolini with ham; gnocchi; Dover sole alla Mugnaia; veal piccatine al limone; calf's liver alla Veneziana; Napoleon with vanilla cream; meringue cake; gelato.

CUT BY WOLFGANG PUCK (STRIP)   Steakhouse

Palazzo
(702) 607-6300
palazzolasvegas.com / wolfgangpuck.com
5:30-11 p.m., daily
$75-$125

Every restaurant in Las Vegas would be a steakhouse if it could be and every steakhouse secretly wishes it were CUT. Steakhouses frame our eating scene like green felt outlines a casino pit, and the numbers these meat emporiums do are staggering. Except for a few slow weeks in summer, this offshoot of the original in Beverly Hills is packed nightly with happy carnivores and meat-craving conventioneers, all ready to blow a car payment on food and a house payment on wine. Having one of the best locations in the world doesn't hurt—a thousand people must walk by the front door every hour—and sourcing some of the best steaks in the business keeps the stiff competition (Morel's on the other side of the casino, Delmonico right around the corner) at bay and punters lined up.

CUT dazzles with its meat (corn-fed, dry-aged, or Wagyu) and everything else it does, including one of helluva cheese cart. As great as those steaks are, I like to swim through the appetizers and sides when I'm paddling around this menu. (For that matter, the seafood is no slouch and the wild-caught turbot is a must if it's on the menu the night you visit.) There's even an argument to be made that you

John Curtas

should park yourself in the bar and partake of addictive chili-lime popcorn, duck-tongue pastrami, or the best mini-sliders you've ever had. Making a meal out of some hot gruyere-coated gougeres and Alaskan king crab rolls isn't bad idea either. (The actual bar is small and tucked in a corner, but the bar room is copious and offers all sorts of seating for sipping or full-scale noshing. In some ways, first-class people watching being one of them, I prefer it to the main dining room.)

The starters set a new standard for steakhouse perfection. Don't miss the warm veal-tongue salad, crab and shrimp Louis, and bone-marrow flan with mushroom marmalade. The maple-glazed ten-spice pork belly will ruin you for any other version (as well as that 20-ounce sirloin you just ordered), and the seasonal salads are fresh, piquant, and balanced. The sides are equally entrancing: tempura onion rings, soft polenta with Parmesan, cavatappi mac and cheese with Quebec cheddar, shaved baby squash with basil in a "bagna cauda" sauce, haricot verts (from some California artisanal angel), and woodsy wild mushrooms like you've never tasted before.

Those steaks, grilled over hardwood and broiler-finished, are as good as you'll find (Wolfgang Puck and Executive Chef Matthew Hurley get the pick of the prime), but if you need a beef break, get the Kurobuta pork chops or rack of lamb.

Desserts are the most ambitious of any steakhouse in Vegas. Before the sweets, however, you must get the cheese. They've assembled a seasonal selection here that is the envy of many a French restaurant. Like everything else about CUT, it's unique and satisfying in ways you didn't think a steakhouse could be.

GET THIS

Alaskan king crab rolls; duck-tongue pastrami; crab and shrimp "Louis"; gougeres; mini-sliders; hand-cut fries; bone marrow flan; roasted turbot; Dover sole, lamb chops; maple-glazed pork belly; veal-tongue salad; dry-aged sirloin; dry-aged rib eye; American Wagyu porterhouse for two; cavatappi pasta mac & cheese; haricot vert; wild field mushrooms; tempura onion rings; cheese cart; cookies and cream baked Alaska; mascarpone-stuffed baked pear; chocolate soufflé.

DISTRICT ONE (WEST) Vietnamese

see map 1, page 233
3400 S. Jones Boulevard, #8
(702) 413-6868
districtonelv.com
Wed.-Mon., 11 a.m.-1 a.m.
$25 or less

Chef/owner Khai Vu is standing Vietnamese food on its ear and creating glamour in a cuisine that used to have all the sex appeal of Hillary Clinton. He's doing this by staying true to the idiom of the country—food rich in fresh herbs, accents, and sour fermented flavors and loaded with contrasts in both texture and aromas—but tweaking it into small sexy plates (and big soup statements) as far from the same old same old as soft-shell crabs are from Mrs. Paul's fish sticks.

Take his Vietnamese carpaccio. Thinly pounded sirloin is stretched provocatively over a rectangular plate, then "marinated" in fresh lime juice and drizzled with sizzling sesame oil. The effect is at once familiar and strange; the oil and acid create a warm salad-like taste and the sliced onions and fried garlic all pop in your mouth with every bite.

Vu doesn't stop there when it comes to mixing his metaphors. Chinese bao (pork-belly buns) are getting as ubiquitous as cheeseburgers, but he gives his a Southeast Asian bent with lightly pickled

John Curtas

daikon and carrot, micro-cilantro, and fresh-roasted and crushed peanuts.

Traditional pho fans might balk, but Vu's lobster pho is worth a special trip and his yellowtail collar is worth two. Perfectly grilled, clean-tasting, soft, buttery, and succulent, it's the apotheosis of this fish, as good as any Japonaise interpretation.

Other standouts include the five-spices roasted Cornish hen and slow-braised pork belly in young coconut juice; each will have your entire table fighting for the last morsel. The groceries used here are a notch or three above District One's competitors and the cooking is more careful, more interesting, and more scrumptious than you'll find in any Vietnamese restaurant in the Mojave Desert.

I used to think all Vietnamese food tasted alike, until Khai Vu showed up on the scene to re-interpret it for me. Even better, he's opened a downtown branch—called Le Pho—where his tasty takes on banh mi, vermicelli bowls, and hoi nan chicken rice are becoming legends in their own right.

GET THIS

Lobster pho; carpaccio of beef; Hue spicy beef noodle soup; the Big Bone soup; bao pork-belly buns; five-spice roasted Cornish game hen; beef and lemongrass wrapped in betel leaves; grilled whole squid; slow-braised pork belly in coconut juice; clay-pot chicken rice.

'E' BY JOSE ANDRES (STRIP)　　　Spanish

Cosmopolitan
(702) 698-7050
ebyjoseandres.com
Tues.-Sun., 5:30 & 8:30 p.m. seatings
$125 and up

My affection for José Andrés is inversely proportional to my dis-like of molecular cuisine. Life is too short to be confused by your food and the whole culinary sleight-of-hand that was all the rage a decade ago is pretty much played out by now. But if you let your guard down, this six-year-old restaurant-within-a-restaurant (Jaleo) will win you over with passion and precision for tweezer food that turns out to be a ton of fun. By way of comparison, if you've ever endured the humorless three-hour slog that is dinner at Alinea, you know how tedious modern food can be. Here, they keep things breezing along and send home 16 diners a night with big smiles on their faces.

Once you score a reservation (done online and not as hard as it sounds, although it may take a week or two to bag a couple of seats), walk into the sanctum sanctorum and hang on tight. What you're in for are 25+ courses of the most dazzling cooking you're likely to find anywhere in America. It's a hoot of an experience, a must for any ardent foodie. It's definitely not for traditionalists, or someone who demands large proteins with his evening meal, or those who

　　　John Curtas

like a few carbs with their foamy this and immersion-circulated that. (There are practically none.)

What you'll also get, if you're lucky, are the sweetest clams you'll ever taste under espuma (foam), molecular olives that are still a treat (no matter how many times you've had them), and an Ibérico ham soup that is as odd and intense a broth as you'll ever experience. Man does not live by molecule manipulation alone, so expect gorgeous fish and meat courses to round out your meal and meld perfectly with the (mostly Spanish) wines chosen for the occasion.

From what I've observed, the average customer for this experience is an upper-middle-class Gen-X gastronaut, for whom this sort of experience is a necessary station on the cross of their gourmet education. Aging Boomers may consider all this molecular folderol to be the equivalent of kids playing in a gastronomic sandbox, but take heart: You will still be blown away by five chefs employing every trick in the book to satisfy and sate your culinary curiosity.

GET THIS

There is no ordering, so whatever they're making is what you'll get. With any luck, you'll be served José's sangria; beet gazpacho; José's tacos; oyster and oyster; Ibérico ham soup; clams in orange espuma; Spanish pizza; morels en papillote; fluke with caviar; crema Catalana egg; rib eye beef cap; plus a dozen other eye-popping creations.

EATT GOURMET BISTRO (WEST)   French

see map 2, page 234
7865 W. Sahara Avenue, #104-105
(702) 608-5233
eattfood.com
Mon.-Sat., 11:30 a.m.-5 p.m.; Mon.-Thurs., 5-8:30 p.m.;
Fri. & Sat., 5-9:30 p.m.
$25-$75

When EATT Gourmet Bistro opened its doors a year ago, I was less than confident in its chances for success. The location on West Sahara had been the graveyard of a number of places, ranging from health food to barbecue, and the name it began with (EATT Healthy Food) inspired neither optimism nor appetite.

What the place had in spades, though, was the faith of its owners. The three of them (chefs Yuri Szarzeweski and Vincent Pellerin, along with manager Nicolas Kalpokdjian) exuded the confidence of youngsters who didn't know what they were getting into.

Szarzweski and Pellerin trained with some of the best chefs in France and their technical proficiency is impressive, including some pretty high-flying recipes. On the other hand, I'm concerned that they're perhaps too good for the 'burbs; it's well-known that most Las Vegans favor familiar food at bargain prices, and familiar this food is not.

There's nothing ordinary about gorgeous cantaloupe "roses" accented with balsamic crisps or octopi carpaccio of uncommon

42   John Curtas

awesomeness. Medallions of glazed pork in a pea purée are a tough sell off the Strip. The neighborhoods of Las Vegas have never seen anything like a supple duck breast atop a silky corn purée dotted with fresh blueberries, baby corn, and popcorn—a dish that sounds a bit odd, looks a bit strange, and tastes a bit more than wonderful.

Seasonal eating is something to which most neighborhood joints only give lip service. At EATT, you get not one seasonable soup, but two: a cold asparagus and a gazpacho in summer, both so vibrant with veggies you're tempted to order a second bowl and forget about the rest of your meal altogether. The seasonal vibe carries through the entire menu, from the martini glass of king crab to the beautifully composed burrata with cubed tomatoes and pesto. As for Pellerin's desserts, top to bottom, they're just about perfect.

This is sophisticated food to be sure, the most refined cooking by far anywhere outside of a major hotel. In many ways, it reminds me of a more casual, slightly less refined version of Twist by Pierre Gagnaire.

Healthy, eye-popping, inventive, French food, on West Sahara at Buffalo. Who would've thunk it five years ago?

GET THIS

Cold asparagus soup; goat-cheese tartine; octopus carpaccio; salmon and tuna ceviche; beet salad; king crab cocktail; ratatouille; burrata with pesto; cantaloupe with balsamic crisps; pork with pea purée; duck breast with blueberries; whatever is in season; whatever Vincent Pellerin is cooking up for dessert.

EDO GASTRO TAPAS & WINE [WEST]   Spanish

see map 1. page 233
3400 S. Jones Boulevard, #11A
(702) 641-1345
edotapas.com
5-11 p.m., daily
$25-$75

Edo's matchbox dimensions (in the old Chada Thai space) belie an attempt to expand the flavors of Spain beyond all boundaries. By and large it succeeds, in a 40-seat room that announces from the get-go you're in for a wild ride in tapas territory.

Similarly, it looks unassuming from the front, but it has quite a pedigree. Exec Chef Oscar Amador Edo is a Strip veteran, while partner Roberto Liendo (late of Bazaar Meat) runs the front of the house. They have a strong sense of what appeals to gastronauts who demand the new over the tried and true. And while the whole small plates/tapas thing may seem like old hat by now, they freshen the genre by blending the traditional with more than just a nod to their Asian surroundings.

Four different dressed oysters are offered—depending on what sort of bath you like your bivalves to take: tamarind mole with pickled cucumber or kiwi leche de tigre, to name two. They're all fabulous. Just as tasty, if a bit run-of-the-mill these days, are the obligatory Spanish cheese-and-ham selections. This is not to damn Spanish jamón with faint praise—it's the tastiest cured pork leg in the world—but only to point out that these folks get their stuff from the same distributors as everyone else, so if you've chowed down on one lomo, you've probably tasted them all. The really expensive hams are too dear for our 'burbs and you'll have to head to Bazaar Meat (and pay through the snout) for them.

John Curtas

As satisfying as these starters are, Edo hits his stride with the cold and hot tapas. His fermented tomatoes with burrata and basil air is probably the most summery dish you can have when the mercury tops 100. It both sparkles and soothes the palate the way only super-sweet *tomates* can, making like an overripe Caprese at half the weight. While his tuna tostada is a little bland, the big and chunky Maine lobster comes salpicón-style, dressed with more of that "tiger's milk" that nicely lightens the richness of the crustacean.

On the hot-tapas side, just pick and point: croquetas with kimchi pisto; pulpo viajero (octopus with tamarind mole), buñelos de bacalao (salt-cod fritters with squid ink and lime), and something called "Bikini" (wafer-thin crispy sobrasada and Mahon cheese) that might be the last word in tiny toast. You can't go wrong with any of the plates here; some are just more spectacular than others.

Among the more eye-popping ones are huevos estrellados, olive-oil fried eggs and piquillo peppers atop a melange of mushrooms and fried potatoes. Top it off with some garlic-parsley oil and you have a classic of Spain tweaked in all the right ways.

The menu is balanced between meat and seafood, but even the seafood can have a certain dense rich sensibility, such as when Manila clams are given the full arroz meloso de pescadores (rice seafood stew) treatment. The paella is worth a trip all by itself.

None of the new tapas places goes overboard on desserts and this is a good thing. After bombarding your senses with oysters, clams, eggs, ham, and octopus, you're looking for something simple and soothing. The flan here pushes all the right buttons and the olive-oil dark-chocolate fudge does the same while adding an inch to your waistline. To go lighter, you'll love the intensity of the strawberry granita with popcorn mousse.

GET THIS

Oysters; ham and cheese platter; fermented tomatoes with burrata; lobster salpicón; croquetas with kimchi pesto; pulpo (octopus) with tamarind mole; buñelos de bacalao (salt cod fritters); "Bikini"; huevos estellados; piquillo peppers; rice-seafood stew; paella; dark-chocolate fudge; granita with popcorn mousse.

ELIA AUTHENTIC GREEK TAVERNA (WEST)   Greek

see map 2, page 234
4226 S. Durango Drive
(702) 284-5599
elialv.com
Mon.-Sat., 11:30 a.m.-10 p.m.;
Sun., noon-9 p.m.
$25-$75

Is there anyone who doesn't take false advertising by restaurants for granted? How many times have you just shrugged when you saw "homemade" on a menu or "Voted Best" on a sign? So inured am I to the hyperbole of food puffery that I barely blink when something tells me that some foodstuff is the greatest this, the most authentic that, or the healthiest the other. Most of the time, most of us presume the exact opposite of what's being touted and no one bats an eyelash.

When it comes to "authentic" Greek food, as Elia claims in its name, most Greek restaurants are co-conspirators against consumers and the land of their birth. Like the Chinese and Italians before them, these immigrants created facsimiles of recipes that dumbed down the real thing. Why? Why else? Because, they thought, and rightly at the time, Americans couldn't handle the truth.

However, unlike other ethnic restaurateurs who simply watered things down, Greeks have invited entire countries into their kitchens. Thus, you can often find everything from mezze platters (Persia) and falafel (Syria) to hummus (Israel), Caesar salads (America), and kebabs (Turkey) in your average Greek restaurant. Imagine French chefs cooking up a passel of pizza, bratwurst, and bangers in a bistro and you'll get the idea. The bastardization of the real food started decades ago and it shows no signs of abating, as most Greek now gets compromised by a lava flow of babaganoush and enough shingles of pita bread (Lebanon) to tile a roof.

John Curtas

Amidst our raging Aegean Sea of mediocrity is an island of Hellenic serenity. With nary a cliché in sight, Elia Authentic Greek Taverna opened its doors recently and immediately started changing people's preconceptions about this cuisine. No Greek flags fly. No hideous Greek statuary adorns. The color scheme is not another variation of bright blue and white. The walls are muted, the linens are thick, and the tablecloths are real cotton. Even the bouzouki music is tuned to a nice conversational level. In short, this small 30-seat space is unlike any American-Greek restaurant you have ever been to.

Small it may be, but mighty are what come out of this kitchen. Whole fish, supple grilled octopus, gorgeous oregano-dusted lamb chops, oven-roasted lemon potatoes, superb tomato salad, gigante beans, and the big four of savory dips (tzatziki, tarama, tyrokafteri, and skordalia) all pay homage to the kind of food that Greeks themselves take for granted at home or in the neighborhood taverna. The all-Greek wine list is well-priced and the welcome makes you feel like you belong—because you do and because real Greek food finally does in America. The only untrue thing about Elia is that it's not located on a side street in Athens.

GET THIS

Greek salad; dolmades (stuffed grape leaves); kolokythakia (fried zucchini); savory dips (skordalia, tyrokafteri, tarama, tzatziki); pork gyro sandwich; gigante beans; grilled octopus; spanokopita (spinach and cheese pie); meatballs; roasted feta cheese; lamb chops; Greek potatoes; whole fish; souvlaki; Greek hamburger; galataboureko (semolina custard in phyllo).

ESTHER'S KITCHEN (DOWNTOWN)   Italian

see map 1, page 233
1130 S. Casino Center Boulevard, #110
(702) 570-7864
estherslv.com
Mon-Fri., 11 a.m.-3 p.m.; 5-11 p.m., daily; Sat. & Sun., 10 a.m.-3 p.m.
$25-$75

   In less than two years, Esther's has become so populat that a seat at the bar (any night of the week) is harder to find than a Mario Batali fan, Esther's is Ground Zero for downtown's dining renaissance. Don't be deterred, though; all this means is you should time your arrival carefully, before the downtown denizens descend.

   What began with Carson Kitchen four years ago took a giant leap forward in 2018 when chef/owner James Trees opened this 80-seat space just off Main Street in the Arts District. But where CK is all gas-tropub-y with its burgers, salads, wings, and such, Trees goes full Italian, bombarding you with antipasti, verduras, pastas, and pizzas straight from a Roman's playbook. He even throws in a fish of the day (always worth it), brick chicken (a crowd favorite), and porchetta (never as good as I want it to be).

   Another thing CK and EK have in common is ear-splitting military-jet afterburner noise levels. Be forewarned: This is not a place for intimate (or even business) interactions. My solution is to come either for a late lunch or an early dinner or, weather permitting, sit outside.

Begin with the bread, because it's baked in-house and out of this world. Then proceed to the meat and cheese platter, one of the prettiest in Vegas. From there, dive into the verduras (veggies): cauliflower with anchovy, chili, garlic, and capers; mushrooms with house-ground polenta; an above-average Caesar; and a chopped salad so enticing everyone at your table will grab a forkful. At lunch, you'll love most of the sandwiches, with the grilled truffle cheese with mushroom, on house bread crusted with fontina cheese, attaining second-level status in the pantheon of grilled fromage. The garlic poached-tuna Niçoise Things is too healthy for me (and occasionally underdressed), but the Spicy Greens with candied pecans, pickled (and I mean pickled) plums, brie, and prosciutto hits just the right balance between produce, spicy, and sweet.

As good as the left side of the menu is, the pastas and pizzas are where the kitchen really shines. Trees is a veteran of the Los Angeles restaurant wars and he knows a thing or two about how to grab a diner's attention. The spaghetti pomodoro, chiatarra cacio e pepe (with pecorino cheese and black pepper), bucatini all'amatriciana, and rigatoni carbonara are handmade, portioned for two, and presented to elicit oohs and aahs for Trees' perfection of pasta porn.

Where you'll really gasp, though, is when you see his radiatorre with black garlic, lemon, and cream, a palate-coating belly bomb of the best kind.

Pizzas are far from standard issue either, with beautiful charred cornicione, good cheese, and always a surprise or two in the topping department, like salty bacon with caramelized onions or Greek sausage and fennel.

All of it amounts to Italian comfort food for the 21st century. It may not be like any Roman trattoria I've ever been in, but with a significant cocktail program, amazing amaros, and a wine list where everything is $40 (by the bottle, not glass), it's a modern American version that seeks to do the same thing: feed its customers in a way that will have them returning again and again.

GET THIS

Sourdough bread; meat and cheese platter; polpette (meatballs); spaghetti squash with ricotta salata; little gems salad; chopped salad; Caesar salad; cauliflower with anchovy; all pastas, but especially the radiatorre with black garlic and bucatini all'amatriciana; all pizzas, but especially the margherita and the bacon and egg; market fish; brick chicken.

ESTIATORIO MILOS (STRIP)   Greek

Cosmopolitan
(702) 698-7930
cosmopolitanlasvegas.com
11:30 a.m.-3 p.m., daily;
Dinner: Sun.-Thurs., 5-10:30 p.m.; Fri.-Sat., 5-11:30 p.m.
$75-$125

The fresh fish selection here is as stunning as the bill you'll receive for it, but don't let that deter you. What's on your plate will cost a pretty penny, but that's only because you're paying for these Aquarians to taste as fresh as they did when they were lifted from the Mediterranean Sea less than a day before.

Everyone starts with the Milos special, a fried tower of zucchini chips with tzatziki and fried cheese, but you can't go wrong with the crudo (raw fish), tomato and feta salad, or any of those creamy or earthy dips (taramosalata, skordalia) that the Greeks do better than anyone. They've given up trying to teach people to say avgotaraho, and list this cured mullet roe under its more familiar Italian name: bottarga. No matter what you call it, the Greek version beats any you'll find in any Italian restaurant on these shores. When fresh Portuguese sardines are available, you should get them, and when you see the bright red Carabinieros shrimp, you should suck some sherry out of their decapitated heads like good Greeks and Spaniards do. They're not cheap, but the experience—again, costly though it is—is memorable, tasting like the richest lobster bisque you've ever had.

It's easy to go on about the fish here and what I'm raving about might not be available when you visit, but whatever is will be impeccable, grilled whole, de-boned, and served in the simplest of ways. Greek fishermen think a sprig of seasoning and a squeeze of lemon is all a great fish needs to show its best and that philosophy informs this menu. That said, an entire milokopi, encased and baked in a salt crust, is a mighty impressive way to lock in the flavor of these sublime swimmers.

Landlubbers won't be disappointed in the superb steaks and lamb chops off these grills and vegetarians will have no trouble chowing down on the plant matter they season and treat with respect.

Greek wines fit this food like feta cheese and phyllo and the list here is impressive and (relatively) affordable. Don't even try to pronounce them, just ask the expert sommeliers for guidance and a language lesson.

No mention of Milos is complete without a plug for the $30 three-course lunch. It's by far the best way to experience this cuisine without breaking the bank and it's proved so popular that reservations, or an early arrival, are mandatory if you want to snare a seat.

About the only thing I don't like about Milos are the desserts. There's nothing wrong with them (yogurt and fruits, baklava, and the like), they're just boring, even by Greek standards.

GET THIS

Carabinieros shrimp; crudo Greek tomato salad; Milos special; Maryland crab cake; sardines; grilled octopus; taramosalata dip; avgotaraho (bottarga); Milokopi fish in salt crust; fresh whole fish; lavraki (Mediterranean sea bass); fried barbounia (red mullet); Dover sole; Greek potatoes; grilled vegetables; herb couscous; lunch special.

FERRARO'S ITALIAN RESTAURANT (EAST)   Italian

see map 1, page 233
4480 Paradise Road
(702) 364-5300
ferraroslasvegas.com
Mon.-Fri., 11:30 a.m.-3 a.m.; Sat.-Sun., 5 p.m.-3 a.m.
$75-$125

I've eaten at Ferraro's more times than I can count. I ate here in its pre-great-wine-list phase, its "the-only-good-Italian-restaurant-in-town" phase, its pink-neon phase, and its "let's-move-closer-to-the-Strip" phase. I've seen Ferraro's through so many phases, you'd think it was one of my unruly children. Sometimes it's felt like one.

For 32 years I've loved this place, but I haven't always been in love with it. These days, I *am* in love with it. That's because, a couple of years ago, an Italian Renaissance of the most delicious kind took place on Paradise Road. That was when the Ferraro family—Calabrians by birth and temperament (i.e., fiery)—had the good sense to put a Sicilian (no shrinking violets themselves) in charge of the kitchen. Francesco di Caudio thus turned a restaurant that's been good for decades into one that's great, by bringing some southern swagger and attention to detail to the kitchen. Di Caudio prepares sausages in house, cooks an Apulian burrata with mushrooms to die for, serves trippa satriano that makes the family proud, and does things with tagliarni with Castelmagno cheese that would put a Milanese into a swoon. Everyone gets the osso buco (and it's great), but the coniglio brasato (braised rabbit with soft polenta) is the dish to try. The pasta dishes are full of swagger and even the simple cacio e pepper spaghetti will have you wondering if noodles can taste any better.

Ferraro's has always had a good wine list. About a dozen years ago, it started having a great one. Now, it has a *lista dei vini* that might be one of the best Italian lists in the country. Even better is the fact that paterfamilias Gino loves to discount amazing obscure bottles of serious wine to keep his inventory moving. (If you want to quibble with the wine program, you might wish the by-the-glass offerings were a bit more inventive.)

But quibbles will quickly be quashed after one bite of di Caudo's sardines, or his silky-smooth tomato risotto, or a calf's liver in red wine that will make you weep. Whatever phase this one turns out to be, I hope it stays in place for a long while.

GET THIS

Trippa satriano; tortellini; osso buco; gnocchi pomodoro; polpettine (meatballs); Apulian burrata with mushrooms and artichoke; carpaccio; house-made sausage; spaghettini aglio e olio; manzo tonnato; risotto; braised rabbit; pappardelle mimmo; tiramisu; lots and lots of red wine.

HATSUMI (DOWNTOWN)

Japanese

see map 1, page 233
1028 Fremont Street, #100
(702) 268-8939
5-10 p.m., daily
$25-$75

You'll notice three things about Hatsumi as you approach it: 1) the strange slightly forbidding neighborhood; 2) the walled-off fortress that encases it; and 3) its nondescript entrance. None of these gives you a clue that a sensational roba-tayaki/yakitori restaurant (operated by a bunch of *gaijin*, no less) lies within. Take the plunge, pilgrim, because excellent eats beckon at Ferguson's Motel—the Downtown Project's latest uber-cool real estate venture—courtesy of Dan Krohmer, one of our most successful local chefs (see Other Mama).

Once you enter the restaurant, things start to make sense. The skinny room is situated sideways, with the open kitchen and bar just a couple of steps from the doorway. To the left and right are comfortable booths, and what at first seems odd quickly becomes surprisingly comfy and welcoming.

Krohmer's other restaurant, Other Mama, is all about seafood and he's received much local acclaim for his unique spin on sushi, crudo, and all things swimming. With Hatsumi, he's ditched the fish *yanagi* (knife) for a barnyard *yaki* (grill) in order to marinate, skewer, and quickly cook a host of bite-size Japanese delicacies, the sort of quickly consumed food you find underneath train tracks all over Tokyo.

Before you get to those skewers, however, you should first head straight to the okonomiyaki, a savory cabbage pancake spiked with shrimp and bacon that pushes all the right umami buttons. Then

John Curtas

proceed to the breaded and deep-fried eggplant katsu, which will have even eggplant haters reflexively grabbing for second bites. Both of these come under the "Plates" section of the menu and are meant to be shared, as are the gyoza (underneath the crispy latticework cover that's all the rage), beef tataki salad (swimming in *ponzu*), and lomi lomi (ocean trout, also swimming in the chili-enhanced citrus-soy sauce). Less acidic, but equally satisfying, are the poached chicken salad, nicely dressed with mild miso vinaigrette and full of big chunks of cashews, and asparagus chawanmushi, a baked, grainy, white tofu custard that tastes better than it looks. If it's available, get the crispy quail breast stuffed with ground pork and flecked with veggies. Unless you're a tofu lover, skip the house-made stuff—the bland leading the bland. You're better off with the pickled vegetables; they're a lot tastier and a treat unto themselves.

The skewers, lots of them, are grilled carefully over *binchotan* charcoal and glazed with sweet soy. The perfect bar food. For all of its Asian food bona fides, Las Vegas hasn't had a pure yakitori restaurant (specializing in grilling chicken parts) until now. Heart, liver, thigh, skin, meatball, you name it, if it's edible, they'll thread it on a skewer and deliver a compact package of succulent morsels to your table, on point and perfect.

Krohmer's menu is striking in its insistence on hewing closely to the izakaya template. How he carefully articulates the flavors of Japan, without compromise, is something to behold. What you wash it all down with will involve either a cocktail, beer, or sake. (The wine list is practically non-existent, just like in Japan.) The selection of sakes is impressive and priced for all budgets. Bottles are offered in both 300 ml and 720 ml sizes, making light imbibing a breeze if you're a party of one or two. Nothing goes better with this food.

As for dessert, Japanese restaurants are to sweets what French restaurants are to sushi. Skip it and have another sake.

GET THIS

Gyoza; beef tataki; lomi lomi; crispy quail; eggplant katsu; okonomiyaki; asparagus chawanmushi; pork belly with turnip kimchi; skewers, skewers and more skewers, especially: miso chicken breast, skin, heart, meatball, thigh, and liver; pork belly, beef tongue; veal sweetbreads, lamb leg, beef filet, okra, eggplant, quail.

JALEO (STRIP)

Spanish

Cosmopolitan
(702) 698-7950
jaleo.com
noon-5 p.m., daily; Dinner: Sun.-Thurs., 5-11 p.m.; Fri.-Sat., 5-midnight
$75-$125

The paella pit alone is worth the price of admission. On it lies a rectangular grill fronted by several small bonfires that blaze away underneath pans the size of manhole covers. In these pans are the purest smokiest expression of Spain's most iconic one-dish meal. If you're the sort who gets excited by these things, you can stand and watch the flames lap up the sides of steel loaded with various proteins and veggies on their way to becoming the best paella in America.

You can sit at the highboy tables beside the pit or at the cocktail bar. Or hunker down in the large low-ceiling room at one of the low-slung banquettes and pick from a variety of gin and tonics, practically the Spanish national cocktail. Wherever you sit, you'll be treated to the ongoing action of the fires and cacophony of a tapas bar that never misses a beat. The room mimics the vibe of the original in Washington D.C., but presents as a big Vegas joint that hasn't lost its original point of view, a perspective that embraces the foods of Spain, both traditional and modern.

This attitude is informed by the force of nature of its celebrity

John Curtas

chef, José Andrés. Andrés doesn't so much cook as he inspires, cheerleads, and imbues ThinkFoodGroup (the corporation behind him) with a passion for quality that most other celebrity-chef outlets never approach.

It's impossible to get bored with Andrés' food. The menu is so varied and the quality is so high that pointing and picking are half the fun. If there's a first among equals in the tapas, it's the tomato bread—crusty rough slices on which fresh tomatoes have been grated into a pulverized mass of sweet flesh and juice. It's the simplest sounding thing in the world, but when done right as it's done here, it will send your palate into spasms of satisfaction. The same bread contributes to the best tuna-salad sandwich you've probably ever eaten and you won't find a better goat-cheese salad or gambas al ajillo, shrimp with garlic, on any $25 (for three courses) lunch menu anywhere. No one makes a better gazpacho or patatas bravas, and the hanger steak is the envy of many a steakhouse.

I like to come at lunch when the douchebags and bachelorettes are in fewer supply. The time definitely not to go is on a weekend evening when both food and service are stressed to the max. Whenever you do, get a G&T and that paella and by all means, fill up on tomato bread.

GET THIS

Paella; molecular olives; gin and tonics; sangria; gazpacho; pan de cristal con tomate fresco (tomato bread); José's tuna sandwich; boiled octopus with peewee potatoes; shrimp and lobster fritters; patatas bravas; gambas al ajillo (shrimp with garlic); hanger steak; Iberico ham/sausage selection; endive and goat-cheese salad; salmon with Manchego pisto.

JOEL ROBUCHON (STRIP)   French

MGM Grand
(702) 891-7925
mgmgrand.com
Mon.-Sat., 6-10:30 p.m.
$125 and up

Having a Joël Robuchon restaurant in your hotel is like having a Vermeer hanging in the lobby or Yo-Yo Ma playing in the house band: Most people will walk right by and not know what they're missing. The cognoscenti, however, will thank their lucky stars. That's the way it is with quintessence. Most of the world wouldn't appreciate it if it bit them on their artisanal ass.

Imagine being so good at something that the only competition you have is with yourself. Every day, the air you breathe is rarified; the tasks you perform are unparalleled in your industry, save for a handful of similarly gifted colleagues strung across the globe. Then imagine that your toils take place within a soulless environment, populated by slack-jawed Philistines, sharp-eyed grifters, and bulbous middle-managers. Your town practically ignores you and, except for a handful of high rollers and black-belt foodies, you're invisible. Nevertheless, you persevere in a corner of behemoth casino and perform at a level of craftsmanship almost unequaled anywhere in the world.

Such is the role of Joël Robuchon in Las Vegas. On any given night, it's one of the best restaurants in the known universe, existing solely to provide a certain level of luxury for MGM patrons and destination dining for those gastronomes with the perseverance (and coin) to find it.

Robuchon the man (who died in 2018) and the restaurant represent a level of high-toned fanatical perfectionism that's impressive even by French haute-cuisine standards. Nowhere but here will you find a bread cart so elaborate, the amuse bouche so precise, butter so luscious, or proteins so refined. The good news is all of these can now be enjoyed during something less than a culinary forced march. A variety of four- to five-course menus run well below the $455 degustation and allow garden-variety gourmets to enjoy this cooking in a two-hour time frame, and at a $150-$250/pp price range. Steep it still may be, but the climb isn't so daunting and the payoff is more than worth it.

What you get will be seasonal, extracted, and intense. Chilled corn soup makes you wonder how corn could be so silky. Morels and asparagus atop an onion jam tart ask how can vegetables taste so much of themselves and yet even more? Foie gras in whatever guise will make your knees weak and however they're stuffing noodles (with truffled langoustines, perhaps?) will redefine your idea of how delicate a pasta can be. They have fabulous beef here (and, of course, beautiful duck), but seafood is the thing, whether it's scallops in green curry, a flan of sea urchin, or John Dory under a shield of tempura shiso leaf. Placing a soft-boiled egg in a light Comte cheese sauce topped with an Iberico ham crisp is so good it ought to be illegal.

Commanding this brigade de cuisine is Christophe De Lellis who, despite his youth, brings an artisan's hand and a general's authority to the proceedings. At this level of cooking, mistakes are something other kitchens make.

You won't be able to resist dessert or the petit-fours cart, so don't even try. I give Robuchon's cheese cart the nod over Guy Savoy's by the width of a ribbon of Tête de Moine.

The Great Recession did for this wine list what my last divorce did for my sex life: improved it immeasurably with lots more variety at different price points.

GET THIS

Four- and five-course menus; degustation menu (for tri-athletes with time on their hands); chilled corn cream soup; asparagus velouté; morel-asparagus tart; boiled egg with Comte sauce; sea-urchin flan; truffled langoustine ravioli; frog leg fritter; scallops in green curry; John Dory with tempura shiso leaf; caramelized black cod; spit-roasted duck; grilled wagyu rib eye cap; Robuchon potatoes, all the bread; all desserts; petit fours.

KABUTO EDOMAE SUSHI (WEST)　　　Japanese

see map 1, page 233
5040 W. Spring Mountain Road, #4
(702) 676-1044
kabutolv.com
Mon.-Sat., 6-8:30 p.m.
$75-$125

Kabuto is too good for you. Stop reading right now if you're the sort who's ever swooned over a California roll or had a screaming orgasm over cream cheese and mayonnaise on raw fish. But if you enjoy the real deal—pristine hand-carved slices of exquisite swimmers atop barely warm seasoned rice—then we've got something to talk about.

Real sushi, Edomae (Tokyo-style) sushi, is a relatively new phenomenon. It's only been around a couple of hundred years in Japan and for about three in Vegas. "Edo" is the ancient Japanese word for Tokyo, and it refers to sushi served by the piece, in a serene setting, with mildly vinegared rice and the slightest dab of true wasabi (not that bright green horseradish stuff they smear on in Americanized joints). True sushi can and should be eaten with the fingers. You dip only the fish, ever-so-delicately into the soy, making sure not to sully the rice with all that salt, then pop the whole thing in your mouth. If all of this sounds like an edible form of performance art, congratulations, you're starting to get it.

Real sushi bars are all about the subtle interplay among raw food,

John Curtas

minimalist preparation, the chef, and the customer. They're not about stuffing your face with some inside-out roll containing more ingredients than an episode of "Game of Thrones." If you want to eat sushi like a pro, take a seat and go either the Nigiri Omakase ($48 and perfect for beginners) or the Yoroi (intermediate $80) route. The first one gets you only sliced fish on rice of the highest pedigree, while the second throws in sashimi and faultless grilled items for some variety.

Serious sushi hounds go whole hog with the Kabuto menu ($120) that expands all categories and will keep you nailed to your seat with fascination. Sake, the only thing to drink with this food, is expensive by the bottle and gently priced by the carafe. Anyone who drinks red wine with this food should commit seppuku on the spot.

GET THIS

Nigiri Omakase; Yoroi Omakase; Kabuto Omakase; sake by the carafe.

KAISEKI YUZU (WEST)   Japanese

see map 3, page 235
3900 W. Spring Mountain Road, #A5
(702) 778-8889
kaisekiyuzu.com
Mon.-Sat., 5-10 p.m.
$25-$75

Yuzu may be small, but what it does is a very big deal, indeed. It's not strictly a sushi bar (although there is a small one), and it's not an izakaya in the Raku mold. Instead, it's our most Japanese of restaurants, a place that would be right at home in a Shinjuku alley—serving food so true to the rhythms and tastes of Japan that it's almost shocking when a *gaijin* walks through the door.

Among the many reasons to eat here are the sushi, noodles, and teriyaki bowls, but if you really want to see chef-owner Kaoru Azeuchi strut his stuff, you need to reserve in advance for one of his kaiseki meals. For the uninitiated, *kaiseki* refers to the haute cuisine of Japanese cooking—seasonal eating taken to the nth degree, a multi-course meal that combines the artistry of the chef with a myriad of ingredients, presentations, and techniques. Everything from the garnishes to the plating is thought through and presented in a way to enhance every sense—visual, aromatic, taste, even tactile. Many of the elaborate garnishes are symbolic and all the recipes try to achieve a zen-like communion between the diner and the food.

Azeuchi trained for 16 years as a kaiseki chef in Japan, even hav-

John Curtas

ing the honor of serving the Emperor bestowed on him. Needless to say, you're in good hands.

A typical dinner might start with an appetizer platter containing everything from an ethereal poached egg with caviar to grilled barracuda and uni rice topped with red snapper. From there, a sashimi platter of lobster, striped jack, and halfbeak is equal to anything you'll find on the Strip or at Kabuto or Yui. Then comes the ultimate mushroom soup: a dobin-mushi matsutake broth containing pike conger, cabbage, and shrimp, so startling in its deceptive smoky simplicity that it will spoil you for soup forever.

The full Monty includes six more courses, ranging from grilled ribbons of A-5 Miyazaki Wagyu and steamed scallop cake draped with a latticework of wheat gluten to eel tempura and a "vinegar dish" of seared mackerel that's a bracing combination of tart and smooth.

Like much Japanese food, once you stop looking for in-your-face flavor and start appreciating the nuances, you quickly find that you can't stop eating it. Here, you're treated to an education in the centuries-old traditions in the Land of the Rising Sun: the reverence for seafood, the harmony of vegetables, and the keen awareness of the seasons—everything that Las Vegas is not. This is eating as a form of secular religion and if you're open to the experience, you'll be transported in a way that no other Western meal can match.

The kaiseki at Yuzu is not a formal affair, but because Kaoru-san flies in many ingredients from Japan, it's necessary to book at least three days in advance. How much you want to spend determines how elaborate it can be. The 10-course 16-dish affair we had runs about $175 per person, but for $50 each, you can get a fine introduction to one of the greatest dinners in all of Las Vegas. Some of the simpler kaiseki dishes can be ordered à la carte if you just want to pop in for a quick bite and see what all the shouting is about. Don't miss the sake selection, either. It's the only thing to drink with this food.

Sushi, sashimi, teriyaki bowls; pork shouga yaki combo; chicken karaage combo; tempura special; sashimi special; chicken and egg bowl, yamakake bowl; udon noodles; homemade zaru tofu; housemade yuba (tofu skin); salmon aburi; poke salad; A5 Wagyu Japanese beef; black-pork shabu shabu; cold green-tea soba noodles; ramen nabe tonkotsu soy; dobin-mushi matsutake; kaiseki dinner.

KHOURY'S (WEST)   Mediterranean

see map 2, page 234
9340 W. Sahara Avenue, #106
(702) 671-0005
khouryslv.com
Sun.-Thurs., 11 a.m.-10 p.m.;
Fri.-Sat., 11 a.m.-11 p.m.
$25 or less

I have long admired Khoury's, the Mediterranean/Lebanese restaurant formerly located in the far southwest reaches of the valley. The only thing I didn't like about it was how far it was from my house. Now, it's a bit closer (on West Sahara), having relocated in the past year, and the only thing not to love is how it will spoil you for all other Las Vegas versions of this cuisine. Be forewarned: This city is full of not-so-great Greek/Mediterranean restaurants—a surprising number of which are run by Russians—and industrial gyro meat and tepid tabbouleh are pretty much standard-issue in the 'burbs.

But Khoury's is straight from the old county, in all the best ways. All sausages, pickles, sauces, and pita are made from scratch and the food is aggressively spiced just like they do on the Mediterranean. The house mezze sampler is a nice way to start, and a nice way to feed four to six hungry souls. It's so chock full of goodness (and about a dozen vegetable dishes), you may forget about eating your spiced ground-meat kafta kebabs or the wonderful whole roasted chicken.

Much to the chagrin of my relatives, no Greek in town can top what Khoury's does with fantastic falafel, heavenly hummus, smoky babaganoush, delightful dolmades, luscious loubieh (green beans with garlic and tomatoes), and all sorts of mashed and seasoned cheeses, yogurt, and vegetables. Through it all, you'll be sopping

John Curtas

things up with the never-ending baskets of puffy pita—so light, nutty, and addictive you'll inhale two or three of these Mesopotamian marvels as they get replenished to your table straight from the oven. Try not to fill up on bread, and don't miss the sujuk (spicy sausage) pizza, or lahm bi ajeen (ground lamb pizza), either.

That all of this is done in-house, at easy-to-digest prices (almost everything on the menu is well under twenty bucks, except for the meats), is remarkable. That food can taste this good and be so good for you is a blessing from the food gods.

GET THIS

Lahm bi ajeen; sujuk pizza; tabbouleh; hummus; loubieh (green beans); labni-matoon; mtabal babaganoush (fresh grilled eggplants); mezza platters; bamieh (sautéed okra); whole roasted chicken; dolmades; kafta kebabs; pita bread. Lots and lots of pita bread.

L'ATELIER DE JOEL ROBUCHON (STRIP)　　French

MGM Grand
(702) 891-7358
mgmgrand.com
5-10 p.m., daily
$125 and up

The only thing to dislike about L'Atelier is its infuriatingly incon-
venient location. Unless you're staying in the MGM, to get to it,
you must first endure the worst parking garage on the Strip or pay
through the nose for valet service, run the gauntlet of half-drunk
and poorly dressed tourists (or is it the other way around?), then tra-
verse the length of one of the world's largest and most confusing
casinos. These annoyances pile up quickly when you're hungry and
by the time you actually get to the far reaches of this behemoth of
a building, you can be excused for being in a very bad mood. The
good news is all will be forgiven as soon as you get a whiff of the
place.

The menu can be a bit daunting. There are small bites here and
prix-fixes there, and seasonal menus and degustation suggestions,
and entrées and appetizers that don't fall in either category. There's
even a killer vegetarian menu for those who are so inclined. So,
instead of being intimidated or confused, do what I do: Close your
eyes and point. No matter what shows up, be it flaky cod with eggplant in a dashi broth, the best lobster salad in the universe, a hanger

　　　　　　　　　　　　　　　John Curtas

steak from heaven, or a buttery spaghetti topped with soft-boiled egg, sea urchin, and caviar, you can be assured of a drop-dead-delicious forkful.

L'Atelier, like its big brother Joël Robuchon next door, has been open for 12 years now, and new top toque Jimmy Lisnard (who replaced the beloved Steve Benjamin) has kept things humming along. There is no such thing as perfection—in food or in restaurants—but if a place can be said to put out nearly perfect expressions of the chef's craft, night after night, L'Atelier would be it. I've been here dozens of times and never had a bad meal; I've never even had a bad bite. On second thought, I can almost forgive its inaccessibility. If it was easier to get to, I'd be here every week.

GET THIS

La Morue; flaky cod with eggplant in dashi broth; Le Burger; Ris de Veau (sweetbreads); grilled seasonal vegetables; Les Spaghettis (spaghetti with soft egg, urchin, and caviar); L'Onglet (hanger steak with pommes frites); Le Caille (free-range quail stuffed with foie gras); Le Kampachi (soy-glazed kampachi with endive salad); Le Homard (lobster salad with sherry vinaigrette); Le Jambon (Ibérico de Bellota: Spanish ham with toasted tomato bread). Le Saumon with siracha aioli; eggplant velouté; foie gras parfait with port wine; anything and everything for dessert.

LAMAII (STRIP) Thai

see map 1, page 233
4480 Spring Mountain Rd.,
#700
(702) 238-0567
lamaiilv.com
2 p.m.-2 a.m., daily
$25-$75

Lamaii is playing a different game than many Thai restaurants. Its arena unites highly seasoned food with carefully chosen wines in a slightly more formal setting. Chef/owner Bank Atcharawan has picked up where Chada Street (his previous Thai-meets-wine venue) left off by taking an ice-cream parlor at the far end of a Chinatown strip mall (Sparrow + Wolf anchors the other end) and creating a magical space of comfy booths and upscale furnishings. It isn't luxurious, but it certainly wins the Chinatown design award for comfort, subdued colors, lots of wood, muted lighting, and huge drop-down lamps. (Thai people apparently have a thing for light fixtures the size of hot tubs.)

As pretty as the decor is, it's also gymnasium noisy at peak hours. They also turn the lights too low at night, a problem since they're only open for dinner. Grab a table early if you want to hear yourself think and see your food. What you'll find on your plate (either by touch or flashlight) will blow your socks off, sometimes literally.

You'll first have to negotiate the beverage selections. Atcharawan is an old F&B pro (he previously managed Lotus of Siam), so his lists are full of saison ales, obscure stouts, and obligatory creative cocktails. Regardless of your preferences, there's no ignoring the short wine list. It's an enophile's dream come true, full of interesting bottles at ridiculously low prices.

Atcharawan's cuisine is designed to match with these top-shelf wines and much of his menu dials back the heat in favor of more wine-friendly fare. Loui suan, ground pork wrapped in lettuce and rice paper, is designed to showcase the Thai herbs, not incendiary heat. Pork jowl gets grilled, belly gets deep-fried, chicken is satay'd, and fluffy shrimp cakes the size of ping pong balls float on a plum-blueberry sauce; each is designed to be enhanced by a steely Riesling, luscious Chardonnay, or tangy Sauv Blanc. When the staff asks you how hot you want something, as in the kua gling ground pork with southern curry paste or gang pu (spicy crab curry noodles), strap in and hang on.

No one will ask you how spicy you want your mu pu (crab-fat) fried rice, but the silky richness of rice shot through with crab tomalley doesn't need a pepper kick. Neither does a grilled 12-ounce sua rong hai (rib eye) that might be the best $24 steak in town. The pad Thai here comes festooned with huge crispy prawns and the surprisingly fresh non-muddy-tasting catfish is dressed with perfectly tart chili-lime-mango dressing.

Even the curries are toned down somewhat, but are none the lesser for it. Gang rawaeng, described as an ancient turmeric curry, has the creamy depth to play off fork-tender chunks of braised beef, and that old reliable panang curry gives new life to crackling slices of duck breast. Atcharawan has always done a tongue-searing steak tartare and the one here is for asbestos tongues only.

Everyone gets the honey toast for dessert, but the mango sticky rice, fried bananas, and coconut ice cream are exemplary.

GET THIS

Garlic green beans; loui suan; shrimp cakes with blueberry sauce; steak tartare; gang rawaeng; panang duck curry; pla crispy beef; kua gling; sua rong; mu pu fried rice; pad Thai with shrimp; mango crispy catfish; honey toast; mango sticky rice.

LE CIRQUE (STRIP)

French

Bellagio
(702) 693-8100
bellagio.com
5-10 p.m., daily
$75-$125

If two restaurants can be said to have jump-started our food revolution, Spago and Le Cirque must be given the credit. Spago got the ball rolling in 1992, but Le Cirque's arrival in 1998 caused a seismic shift in our taste tectonics. As good as the rest of Steve Wynn's eateries at Bellagio were (Picasso, Prime, Olives, et al.), he knew he needed a big hitter from the Big Apple to really get the food-world's attention. Enter the Maccioni family, bringing with them what was, at the time, the most famous name in American restaurants.

With the Maccionis patrolling the room and paterfamilias Sirio making constant appearances from New York, Las Vegas was a satellite operation, but every bit the equal of its hallowed namesake. A succession of great chefs has kept this kitchen firing on all cylinders and one of the best service staffs in the business keeps the dining room humming. I was afraid all that might come to an end in 2013 when the management deal with the family ended. With Sirio deep into his eighties now and son Mario gone, the operation is a licensing rather than a management deal—more Bellagio, less Maccioni. The good news is neither the food nor the service has suffered for it.

John Curtas

Credit for that crackerjack service goes to a team that has barely changed in 19 years. If you came here when Bill Clinton was president and returned today, you'd see all the same faces serving you. Frederic Montandon still pours vintages (French, please! California, if you insist) with a twinkle in his eye, while the front of the house is managed like a well-tuned orchestra. A lot of restaurants feel stale after two decades. Not here.

The food has changed over time, but never wavered. Some of the chefs (Poidevin, David Werly, and Wil Bergerhausen) were superstars in their own right, while others were just putting in their time. But whoever was at the helm, the kitchen has always been solid, rendering classics like rack of lamb with glazed sweetbreads and rabbit with mustard cream sauce with the same aplomb it devotes to gold-crusted quail stuffed with foie gras or blue crab under a robe of caviar. You can still get a lobster salad here that is almost note-for-note what Daniel Boulud invented in 1988 or have your taste buds startled by Chris Heisinger's "hidden" spring garden of English peas, tendrils, and garbanzos misted with strawberries.

What used to be dueling menus of Le Cirque classics versus more modern (read: lighter) fare has expanded into four offerings at all price ranges. You can do everything from a $108 pre-theater affair to a $350 extravaganza that steps into the ring with whatever punches Savoy, Gagnaire, or Robuchon are throwing and doesn't flinch. A delicious-sounding five-course vegetarian menu ($115) looks like a good idea, in the same way that yoga classes, wheat grass, and prostate exams do.

Every night seems like New Year's Eve here. High rollers, celebrities, and hedonic jetsetters treat this place like a private club, making a reservation tough on weekends. Personally, I like to go in early mid-week, grab a seat at the bar, and watch the choreography. After almost two decades, the balletic grace of Le Cirque is still something to behold.

GET THIS

Oysters; lobster salad "Le Cirque"; Maryland blue crab with caviar; Savoyard sunchoke soup; foie gras with tapioca; seasonal risotto; braised veal cheeks; roasted chicken; sea bass in potato crust; A5 Wagyu strip with bordelaise sauce; gold-crusted quail farci; rabbit with mustard sauce; sweetbreads; "hidden" spring garden salad; vegetarian tasting menu.

LOTUS OF SIAM (EAST)

Thai

see map 1, page 233
620 E. Flamingo Road
(702) 735-3033
lotusofsiamlv.com
Mon.-Fri., 11 a.m.-2:30 p.m.; 5:30-10 p.m., daily
$25-$75

Yogi Berra once said: "That place is so crowded, no one goes there anymore." Truer words were never spoken about LOS.

Ever since Bill and Saipin Chutima took over this space in 1999, it seems every gourmet in the world has beaten a path to their door. So popular has it become with the fiery-foods crowd that a table is almost impossible to score on a weekend evening—when you'll see taxi after taxi dropping off parties large and small every few minutes as tourists make their pilgrimage here to sample our most famous off-the-Strip eatery.

In no other Thai restaurant in town can you find the variety, freshness, and vivid flavors put forth by this kitchen on a daily basis. (Those who had judged Lotus by its lunch buffet were missing the point of this restaurant. Thankfully, they finally discontinued their tepid ode to the all-you-can-eat-crowd a couple of years ago. These days, if you show up for lunch, which also can be crowded if you don't arrive before noon, you get the same menu as the one served at dinner.) The point of Lotus is and always has been the northern and Issan specialties (all in English on the menu), done the way Saip-

John Curtas

in's mother taught her and well enough to garner her two James Beard Award nominations and (finally), in 2011, the award for Best Chef Southwest (shared with Claude Le Tohic of Joël Robuchon). Pair these dishes with the extraordinary Rieslings that make up one of the best German wine lists in the country.

Add it all up and you have an experience that earns the distinction of being called the best Thai food in the U.S. by Jonathon Gold of the *Los Angeles Times*. Unlike Mr. Gold, I haven't been to every Thai restaurant in the country, but I do tend to agree with him on that score, especially when lingering over bites of Issan sour sausage, koi soi (raw beef with chiles), or Chutima's definitive northern Thai curries. Warning: Gringos should avoid asking for anything "Bangkok hot."

GET THIS

Issan sour sausage; kang hung lay (just because I like saying it); miam kham; khao soi (curry noodles); drunken noodle prawns; catfish larb; nam kao tod (crunchy rice with raw cured pork and peanuts); Panang braised beef; all curries; northern Thai sausage; mango with sticky rice; anything off the northern Thai or Issan menus; any white German or Austrian wine on the phenomenal list, the prices of which are a flat-out steal.

MABEL'S BBQ (STRIP) American

Palms
(702) 944-5931
palms.com
Mon.-Thurs., 11:30 a.m.-10 p.m.; Fri., 11:30 a.m.-midnight;
Sat., 9 a.m.-midnight; Sunday: 9 a.m.-9 p.m.
$25-$75

If I've said it once, I've said it a thousand times: Las Vegas is where barbecue goes to die.

Great 'cue has come and gone over the years. From Struttin' Gates and Paul Kirk's R.U.B. to Salt Lick, all the good ones barely make it two years before pulling up stakes and heading back where they came from. The failures of actual pit-cooked barbecue have rendered the real smoky deal harder to find than a pork chop in a mosque.

I'm a barbecue snob. I've smoked my own meat for years and have traveled to every 'cue corner in this country in search of the meats and pit masters who have turned barbecued meat into an icon of authentic American eats. I even read about smoking meat in my spare time and think nothing of wasting hours on YouTube listening to debates on the merits of hickory versus mesquite and the pros and cons of the Texas crutch. All of which explains why I'm a pretty tough customer when it comes to evaluating the flat end of a brisket or the succulence of some pulled shoulder.

But the times they may be a'changin', thanks to celebrity chef Michael Symon. You might presume that Symon, a Greek-Sicilian

John Curtas

Food Network star from Cleveland, has as much business doing barbecue as dim sum, but like all accomplished chefs, when he sets his mind to cooking something, he does it right.

The brisket is straight out of Austin, targeting that tender, crusty, smoke profile popularized by iconic joints in the Texas Hill country. As good as it is, the Brobdingnagian beef rib will get your attention. Coated with "pastrami spices," it's two-plus pounds of pure, unadulterated, beefy bliss. According to the menu, it's enough for two-plus hungry adults. Realistically, it'll feed four.

Keeping the Texas vernacular going, Symon's hot links have that natural casing snap, toothsome bite, and serious heat you rarely find outside the Lone Star state. Taking a cue (pun intended) from the Carolinas, you can start your meal with crackly/crunchy pig tails, ears, and skins.

Just as Carolina-like is Symon's spicy pulled-pork sandwich, a thing of beauty in its own right, studded with jalapeños and sauerkraut. There are also Kansas City burnt ends, Memphis ribs, and Cleveland-style kielbasa and pastrami-spiced pork belly. When you're done with those, there's plenty more to tackle, including truly sour kraut, housemade pickles, pit beans, hot greens, a very good poppy-seed slaw, and a spiced mac 'n cheese that's a gooey delight. Put it all together and you have a best-hits barbecue restaurant, a something-for-everyone meat fest.

If you're a sauce freak (and let's face it, who isn't?) five are offered: Cleveland Mustard, K.C. Sweet and Sour, Texas Hot, and Green Chile. They all do a great job of honoring their forefathers and even the Alabama White (something of an oddball outlier in the barbecue-sauce lexicon) is a horseradish-lover's dream come true.

The beer list is as impressive as the wine list is paltry. Desserts are limited (floats, bread pudding, ice-cream sandwich), but in keeping with the theme, they're loaded with all kinds of things that will send you to an early grave—with a smile on your face. Anyone who orders a salad here has rocks in their head.

GET THIS

Beef rib; pastrami pork belly; Cleveland chopped-pork sandwich; beef brisket; chopped brisket sandwich; Memphis ribs; burnt ends; kielbasa sausage; poppy-seed slaw; mac 'n cheese; Alabama chicken wings; hot links; pig's ears, tails, and skins; bread pudding; ice-cream sandwich.

MARCHE BACCHUS (WEST)   French

see map 2, page 234
2620 Regatta Drive, #106
(702) 804-8008
marchebacchus.com
Mon.-Sat., 11 a.m.-3:45 p.m.; Sun., 10 a.m.-3:45 p.m.
Sun.-Thurs., 4-9:30 p.m.; Fri.-Sat., 4-10 p.m.
$25-$75

A proper lunch in the suburbs is harder to find than a corkscrew at BYU. Las Vegans don't do lunch, not the way New York or Portland does lunch. Las Vegas' professional classes (to the extent they exist) are too busy filling up on Subway sandwiches to think about lunch. (An exotic power lunch at an old law firm of mine consisted of four partners eating cheeseburgers and pontificating to us underlings over iced teas at Red Robin. Good times.) Lunch in Las Vegas is such a sad and desperate affair that people have been known to travel 15 miles from the Strip to an obscure shopping center on a fake lake to find a small red sign tucked in a corner over a modest doorway that says, Marché Bacchus. They do this because this is one of the few places where civilized people dine—as opposed to just pumping fuel into their tanks—at midday.

Before you get to the food, though, you'll have to navigate the wine store. A wall of pinot noir stands to your right and the floor before you is lined with three rows of wooden bins bulging with bottles. A large wine store it's not, but the selections are carefully chosen, with labels galore at every price range, by the owners, Rhonda

         John Curtas

and Jeff Wyatt. Oenophiles will have a field day while lesser imbibers and teetotalers are being led to their seats. No matter where you fall on the alcohol-consumption continuum, you'll be charmed by the setting and décor—so charmed, in fact, that you might adopt this as your favorite off-Strip restaurant before you've even taken your first bite.

Whether you come for lunch, brunch, or dinner, you and your guests will find plenty of solid cooking to choose from. Most of the large menu skews toward classic French-bistro fare (steak frites, escargot "persillade," and the like), but plenty of pastas and salads satisfy the pickiest crowd. Francophiles won't want to miss the croque monsieur, quiche Lorraine, or onion soup; carnivores go ga-ga over the burger and steak tartare; and those who insist on Italian won't find any fault with the bucatini amatriciana or vegetable ravioli. The brunch menu is more egg-centric, but as good as the Benedicts and goat-cheese omelets are, I prefer meatier fare like the truffled grits and beef grillade, the better to go with all those fabulous red wines at your fingertips for only $10 over the retail price. Because of this very gentle pricing policy, MB has made itself the go-to joint for sommeliers and serious sippers, from all over town and all over the country.

The reason I'm going on about lunch is because lunch is the best time to come to MB. The service is more relaxed, the food is just as good, and lingering by the pond and watching the ducks paddle about is the perfect way to while away an afternoon while your co-workers are swooning over Pizza Hut at their desks. There's no better place in southern Nevada to have an affair, entertain Grandma, drink wine, or play hooky.

GET THIS

Charcuterie platter; cheese platter; French onion soup; quiche Lorraine; escargot "persillade"; croque madame; truffled grits & beef grillades; Prince Edward Island mussels; goat cheese napoleon; steak tartare with quail egg; steak frites; bucatini amatriciana; vegetable ravioli; honey-spiced glazed duck breast; bistro chicken; buckwheat crêpes; Bacchus omelette; smoked salmon Benedict; Bacchus bread pudding.

MATTEO'S RISTORANTE ITALIANO (STRIP) Italian

Venetian
(702) 414-1222
venetian.com
11 a.m.-11 p.m., daily; Brunch: Fri.-Sun., 11 a.m.-5 p.m.;
Lounge: noon-11 p.m., daily
$75-$125

Matteo's aims to take you on a culinary tour of Italy in an easily digestible fashion. It has neither the pedigree of Cipriani nor the ambition of Vetri, but what it does it does well, at a friendly price point.

Your first sign of how good the food is comes from the wine list—well-chosen imports priced to drink, rather than rip off the rubes and soak the high rollers. Most are listed by grape varietals, with plenty in the $50-$100 range. You won't find any bargains, but neither will you need a proctologist after ordering from it.

The next thing you'll notice is the olive oil—not the run-of-the-mill half-rancid stuff put out by Italian restaurants everywhere. This is the real deal from Liguria, with herbaceousness to burn and a soothing back-of-the-throat peppery finish that lasts until next Tuesday. The accompanying white bread is bland (just like in Italy), the better to carry all those earthy notes coming from the oil.

While lapping up that awesome olive oil, you confront the menu. Things you've never heard of (ortolana, peperú, sorentina, mandilli di seta) sit beside those you have (carpaccio, frittura, pappardelle, branzino). Don't despair, everything has complete descriptions in English. My guess is that giving each dish its native name is to inform diners that they're not in Chicken Caesar Salad Land anymore.

A dozen starters cover the Italian map. Pleasant surprises abound: sweet and spicy soft-cheese-stuffed peppers (peperú), bright fresh field greens with watermelon radish and champagne vinaigrette (ortolana), and beer-battered leeks with chickpea fritters (frittura).

One not to miss is the prosciutto, thin slices of sweet-salty ham beneath a mound of stringy-creamy stracciatella cheese, speckled with pepper and drizzled with that insanely great oil. The crispy-fried sage dough on the bottom makes for a picture-perfect amalgam of crunchy, creamy, salty, and sweet. The most expensive antipasti ($25) feeds four as an appetizer. The other starter you must try is the sorentina, Chef Angelo Auriana's homage to the seafood salads of southern Italy, calamari, chickpeas, and fava beans with just the right spark of chili in the lightly applied dressing.

Most of the dishes sound more complicated than they are, but there's nothing simple about plancha-roasted octopus with garbanzo purée and cotechino sausage. The tricks are in using good groceries and knowing how to balance flavors. Once you get to the pastas, you'll realize how well Auriana and his on-site lieutenant, Eduardo Pérez, have mastered this craft.

The signature mandilli di seta (handkerchief-flat noodles in almond-basil pesto) will be a revelation to those who don't while away their time on the Cinque Terre and the seafood ravioli are like pillow-y surprises straight from Naples. The point is: Get as many of the pastas as you can. They're fairly priced ($21-$31), meant to be shared, and as fresh as Genovese basil.

Gorging on those pastas is a worthy endeavor, but if self-control takes hold, save room for the lamb chops, branzino, veal, and 16-ounce rib eye, all superb.

Get the cannolis. They're fantastic. In a class by themselves.

GET THIS

Sweet and spicy peppers; baby greens salad; prosciutto di parma; carpaccio; grilled calamari; beer-battered baby leeks; steak tartare; Ligurian focaccina; corn agnolotti; mandilli handkerchief egg pasta; pappardelle; casonzei pork and veal ravioli; fettucini with Dungeness crab; prosciutto tortellini; branzino; lamb chops; veal rib eye; boneless rib eye; panna cotta; budino pane bread pudding; cannoli.

MICHAEL MINA [STRIP]

Seafood

Bellagio
(702) 693-8865
bellagio.com
Mon.-Sat., 5:30-10 p.m.
$75-$125

I like to call Michael Mina the Egyptian Wolfgang Puck, and he fits the bill for several reasons. First and foremost is his ability to pull off multiple concepts at all price points, while never losing his street cred as one of the most talented chefs in the business. Secondly, while he's serving up everything from sushi (at Pabu in San Francisco) and football fans at 49ers' games to textbook-perfect French classics (e.g., Bardot Brasserie), he never loses sight of the seafood that made him famous. And finally, like Puck, Mina always makes sure his number-one brand is always in top form. With Puck, that would be Spago and with Mina, it's his eponymous restaurants in San Fran and Bellagio. After long runs in both cities, neither seems to miss a beat, and if you stroll into our MM, you'll find it remains as chic and timeless as a Chanel dress.

The Tony Chi design has aged remarkably well and to these eyes is as elegant as ever, remaining one of the most flattering and comfortable rooms in the business. That design does more than just flatter the customers, it also shows off Mina's cuisine to its best effect.

A recent reboot now lets you select from a whole fish display adjacent to the revamped bar and with a new menu, MM and his crew have returned to their roots. Start with the caviar parfait (after 20 years, still one of the best appetizers on the planet), then proceed to the tableside-mixed foie tuna tartare. From there you can pick between hot or cold shellfish platters and whatever fish arrived hours earlier (everything is flown in daily). Fish can be ordered by the whole or half (a nice touch for someone who can't polish off an entire three-pound branzino), and whether you like your Arctic char grilled over applewood or your John Dory broiled and adorned with black beans and scallions, they have you covered.

Landlubbers won't find anything to complain about with Mina's aged New York strip or rib eye "Rossini." Don't plan on skipping dessert either, because missing dessert in a Michael Mina restaurant is like leaving an opera before the fat lady sings.

GET THIS

Tuna tartare, caviar parfait, lobster pot pie; butternut agnolotti; smoked Mt. Lassen trout; hot shellfish platter; cold shellfish platter; crudo of Hamachi, yellowfin, and sea urchin; broiled John Dory; spice-crusted branzino; applewood-grilled Arctic char; rib eye "Rossini"; chocolate bar; pineapple granite

MORDEO BOUTIQUE WINE BAR [WEST]   Latin Fusion

see map 1, page 233
5420 Spring Mountain Rd., #108
(702) 545-0771
mordeolv.com
Mon.-Fri., 11:30 a.m.-2 p.m.; 5-11 p.m., daily
$25-$75

Too many modern restaurants, in their endless quest to mash up American food with every cuisine on the planet, try too hard to dazzle you with their footwork at the expense of harmony and balance. Mordeo never falls into that trap. Both ingenuity and restraint are going on here at the same time, which is rare these days, and the wild ride you take among its flavors will captivate your palate without ever wearing it out. Whereas its competition (Edo and Pamplona) hew closely to Spain, MBWB takes the tapas thing in several different directions and those tangents have as much to do with wine as they do with shareable food. The good news is, both are pretty nifty.

Confronting you when you enter is a long, colorful, in-laid, three-sided bar, representing the latest manifestation of the side-by-side dining that has been all the rage since the late great Robuchon made such a splash with his L'Atelier in Paris in 2003. Grownups may find it a tad awkward and for us, a couple of high-boy tables in one corner can accommodate four to six people who can actually talk without leaning in and out with every sentence. Once you get com-

John Curtas

fortable (and to their credit, the staff here puts everyone at ease), you'll observe the hustle and bustle as all sorts of people move to and fro, taking orders, mixing drinks, pouring wines, and delivering plates. It's really quite a scene, but right out of the chute, the staff and kitchen are well-synchronized. If you score one of those tables, don't expect to hear any whispered sweet nothings from your dearly beloved, though, as that would require a bullhorn over the din. (In this regard, side-by-side seating makes a lot of sense.)

Co-owners Luis de Santos and chef Khai Vu have invented a wine-friendly menu that pushes some boundaries without ever going overboard. Ginormous chicharrones (either plain or topped with jamón iberico—called "the Cloud") provide the perfect nibble to begin your meal. Then it's on to a series of eye-popping plates, such as Beet Garden (red and golden with goat-cheese mousse), a respectable lemony La Ensalada Cesar, and electric-green shrimp agua chile of shocking spiciness. Milder but no less worthwhile are the Maine lobster with mango salsa and lomo lomo ocean trout (a salmon-like ceviche dressed with sesame-chile oil). The meaty king crab leg (at $38, the most expensive thing on the menu) is crabby enough for two, while the cold briny oysters and ginormous Nigerian prawn also show they're serious about their seafood. Other winners include La Asada (grilled Angus skirt steak with some kick-ass chimichurri sauce) and a stew of clams, chorizo, and mussels that has quite a kick of its own (from the white-wine-sriracha sauce).

As for the wine, it's a small but mighty list with everything priced at way below a Benjamin. They're selling bottles of tempranillo, syrah, and Rioja here for what *glasses* of vino go for on the Strip. The cocktails are pretty cool, too.

Desserts are only two in number (and always in flux), but if the mango rice pudding is offered, don't miss it. You'll have no complaints about the flan, either, but when was the last time you complained about a flan?

GET THIS

Chicharrones; The Cloud; La Ensalada Cesar; shrimp agua chile; beet garden; lomo lomo ceviche; lobster with mango salsa; Nigerian prawn; grilled skirt steak; dry-aged rib eye; clam-chorizo stew; king crab leg; flan; mango rice pudding.

MOTT 32 [STRIP] Chinese

Palazzo
[702] 607-3232
venetian.com
5-11 p.m., daily
$75-$125

Mott 32 is as slick as Peking duck skin and just as satisfying. It's a huge well-financed chain of upscale Chinese, with a casual luxurious vibe and ingredient-forward cooking calculated to appeal to purists and tourists alike. Money talks and there's some big bucks behind this joint.

The glamour drips from every opulent detail. Giant doors off the casino floor lead to a bar area hosting an ocean of top-shelf alcohol. The lighting is muted, but not too much, and the young women dotting the place are as sexy and shiny as lacquered Chinese boxes. Dresses are short, black, and tight, and the cleavage is so profound that this joint's nickname ought to be Mott 32D.

The bases-covering menu has everything from Cantonese dim sum and hand-pulled noodles to Peking duck. Dim sum for dinner is the first sign you're in modern Chinese dining territory and the best-in-Vegas xiao long bao (Shanghainese soup dumplings) come four to an order; try both the traditional pork and hot-and-sour versions—the latter providing plenty of punch.

That duck is the centerpiece of every meal here. Duck doesn't get

John Curtas

any duckier: bronzed brittle skin on perfect slices of deeply flavored meat. But be sure to have at least four people at your table before you order it.

Next to the dim sum and duck, the Pluma Iberico pork gets pushed the most by the staff. It's dense with flavor, a bit sweet, and juicy. Before it arrives, you might want a few smaller plates, like the crispy dried Angus beef.

The triple-cooked Wagyu short rib is big enough for four hungry souls and those not wanting to spring for a whole duck can get some shredded quacker in a duck salad with black-truffle dressing. Lighter appetites will appreciate the wild mushrooms in lettuce cups or thick slabs of deep-fried sesame prawn toast, which redefines this usually bland standard.

Being Cantonese, expensive seafood options abound, none of which (abalone, sea cucumber, etc.) make much sense to Occidentals. But there's plenty to love about the lobster ma po tofu, with its chunks of shellfish swimming with spicy-silky bean curd, as well as the smoked black cod and the poached fish (usually sea bass) floating in a Szechuan pepper broth.

More timid eaters will feel right at home ordering a few old reliables: kung po prawns and General Tso's chicken, each properly spicy and not too sweet, along with the nutty shrimp fried rice.

Desserts will get your attention too. They feature the exotic (Bamboo Green Forest), alongside the classical (mango with coconut rice roll), and even an old bean-paste hater like me found myself slurping the pure white custard-like double-boiled egg white. The pastry chefs at Robuchon have nothing to worry about, but for a Chinese restaurant, these are modern, interesting, and damn tasty.

More than anything else, Mott 32 represents modern Chinese no longer defined by egg rolls, fortune cookies, and orange chicken. Whether you're impressing a date or hanging with a crowd of conventioneers, you won't find any better Chinese food in Las Vegas.

GET THIS

Dim sum; Peking duck; smoked black cod; lobster ma po tofu; Pluma Iberico pork; triple-cooked wagyu short rib; kung pao prawns; General Tso's chicken; wild mushrooms in lettuce cups; shrimp toast; Bamboo Green Forest; mango with coconut.

OH LA LA FRENCH BISTRO (WEST)   French

see map 2, page 234
2120 N. Rampart Boulevard, #150
(702) 222 3522
ohlalafrenchbistro.com
Tues.-Fri., 11 a.m.-10 p.m.; Sat., 5-10 p.m.; Sun., 10 a.m.-2 p.m. & 5-9 p.m.
$25-$75

Great French food is everywhere up and down the Strip, but out in the neighborhoods, a decent escargot is harder to find than a stucco-free house. At Oh La La, however, the service is always fast and friendly, the wine list modest, pure, and approachable, the bread is good, and the foie gras terrine even better. OLL might also have the best steak tartare in town; its combo of gherkins, mustard, and onions hits a flavor profile that takes me straight back to Le Train Bleu in the Gare Lyon in Paris.

There's nothing fancy about OLL, but it's rock solid, the kind of food you can depend on. Of all the top 52 in *Eating Las Vegas*, this one is, indeed, *essential*—to its surroundings, to the spirit of its cuisine, and to lovers of great steak frites.

The restaurant is simplicity itself. Chef/owner Richard Terzaghi has parked his little operation on the corner of a building pad inside one of Summerlin's busiest intersections. You can't see it from the street, but once you're inside, you'll notice a sharp little bar against one wall (which never seems to get much action) and two rows of tables filled with folks who know their Niçoise from their Lyonnaise.

John Curtas

Winners abound all over its menu: frisée salad La Lyonnaise (loaded with lardons), garlicky snails, prawn risotto with Israeli couscous, steak frites, mussels, endive salad, great French fries, and simple satisfying desserts all faithful to the homeland without a lot of fuss. And whenever they post a special, be it a seasonal soup or a lamb stew, I always get it and I'm never disappointed. Mussel lovers will feel the same way about the bivalves, with the poulette (with bacon, onions, and cream sauce) belying any thought that you'll save a few calories with shellfish. Richard's pastas are also heavy on the cream sauces, which is just fine until the Vegas thermometer hits over 100. Lighter by far are his roasted beets with orange, pistachio-crusted goat cheese, and heirloom tomatoes served in a jar with pearl mozzarella and herbs de Provence.

French bistros are all about comfort food and that's what Richard offers his loyal customers. Whether they're popping in for a croque Madame at lunch, a Benedict for brunch, or simply some Gruyère-oozing onion soup, they know it's all as good as France gets in the desert Southwest. These folks also line up for what might be the best fish in the 'burbs: a sole Meunière swimming in proper proportions of nutty delicacy to lemony tartness. It may not have ever seen the white cliffs of Dover, but it's a mighty toothsome (Pacific) flatfish for less than half the price of its pedigreed cousins on the Strip. Meatier appetites will want to tuck into the hachis Pamentier (a ground beef casserole topped with cheesy mashed 'taters) or a whole Cornish game hen cooked (in papillote) and served in its rich broth. They do a decent filet mignon, but the bavette a l'echalotte (flank steak in shallot sauce) is the meat you can't beat. Close your eyes and you'll almost believe you're noshing on the Boulevard Saint-Germain.

GET THIS

Onion soup; charcuterie platter; escargot, beef tartare, baked brie; pistachio-crusted goat cheese; endive salad; salad La Lyonnaise; heirloom tomatoes; roasted beet salad; mussels poulette; sole Meuniere; bavette a l'echalotte; prawns risotto; Cornish game hen; hachis parmentier; chocolate mousse; crème caramel; crème brûlée.

OLD SOUL (DOWNTOWN)   American

see map 1, page 233
495 S. Grand Central Parkway
(702) 534-0999
oldsoul.chefnatalieyoung.com
Lunch: Tues.-Fri., noon-3 p.m.; Dinner: Tues.-Sat., 5 p.m.-9 p.m.
$25-$75

And the winner for Best Food in the Most Obscure Location goes to … Old Soul!

Old Soul is so hidden that you'll congratulate yourself on finding the front door. Once you eat there, this issue disappears; you're too busy enjoying yourself to mind the locale.

The World Market Center is a behemoth complex near downtown containing three intimidating buildings and no retail spaces, save for this single door stuck between darkened windows of one ground-floor corner. Inside the Land of the Giants courtyard, the valet parker points to the modest sign and you stroll in, wondering, like all first timers: Who in the world eats here? (The answer: fans of chef/owner Natalie Young and culinary culture vultures looking for her particular brand of gutsy, elevated, American food.)

Old Soul is capacious and dark, with well-spaced tables, a civilized noise level, oversized art on the walls, old silent movies running on the back wall, and antique furnishings (including mismatched dishware)—the vibe is one of cool comfort, designed to make you forget about what's outside. And as soon as you dive into the food, the whole place starts feeling like an overstuffed sofa you've sunk into and don't want to leave.

The space might be an acquired taste, but Young's food is not. She's a self-taught Strip veteran who found her mojo with the 2012 opening of Eat downtown. She's toggled between high-toned French (Eiffel Tower Restaurant) and steaks (P.J. Clarke's) to superior flapjacks (Eat), but here she's found her wheelhouse: elemental American with a certainty that comes only from a confident chef.

It takes confidence to put liver and onions on a menu. Young knows a lot of people like liver—especially tossed with caramelized onions and given a piquant punch by stone-ground mustard—and that an older crowd (who religiously attend concerts at the nearby Smith Center for the Performing Arts) will appreciate a throwback item given just the right update. Everyone appreciates the same attention given a thick slab of meatloaf—adorned with cauliflower purée, meaty 'shrooms, a splash of tomato concasse, and a dribbling of red-wine jus. Cornish game hen gets some gussying up with the help of a wild-rice pilaf speckled with bits of pickled veggies and a tongue-slapping chimichurri sauce. It's comfort food to be sure, but soothing has never had so much sparkle.

Before you get to these mains (available at lunch and dinner for the same price), I'd advise you to bump into as many starters as your gustatory canoe can handle. Most spectacular of the bunch is a head of roasted cauliflower, studded with pickled raisins and peppers, sprinkled with that chimichurri, and festooned with herbs.

The chicken liver pâté is so smooth and silky, it could give torchons of foie gras a run for their money and the smoked trout with housemade applesauce and chive corn cakes will have you straining for superlatives. After the fried oysters with horseradish aioli, you make plans to return as soon as you leave. Crisp and meaty, one bite will take you straight back to a New England clam shack.

For dessert, get whatever cobbler they've made, and the cherry pie, both a la mode. You've come too far to deny yourself such a sweet release, so give in. You can thank me later.

GET THIS

Fried oysters; smoked trout; squid and prawns; chicken liver pâté; liver and onions; roasted cauliflower; Cornish game hen; meatloaf; pork chops; mini-baked potatoes; braised collard greens; street corn; cherry pie; bread pudding; peach cobbler.

OTHER MAMA (WEST) Seafood

see map 2, page 234
3655 South Durango, #6
(702) 463-8382
othermamalv.com
Sun.-Thurs., 5-10 p.m.; Fri.-Sat., 5-11 p.m.
$25-$75

Location counts, except when it doesn't. Other Mama may be harder to find than a celebrity chef in the kitchen, but that hasn't stopped every galloping gastronome around from zeroing in on this hidden gem, tucked into an invisible corner in a generic strip mall on South Durango. In a matter of weeks after it opened, Dan Krohmer's ode to great seafood went from "Where's/what's that?" to "Let's go" on the lips of every foodie in town. These days, it's practically a hangout for off-duty chefs and F&B professionals, as well as the go-to joint for locals seeking serious shellfish.

Nothing about its obscure locale suggests that you're in for top-flight oysters, Penn Cove mussels, or sashimi-grade scallops when you find it. Nor does the name give you a clue—it sounds like a blues bar, and the retro-louche signage suggests a down-on-its-heels absinthe joint you might find in New Orleans. Even when you walk in, things are bit confusing. It's modestly appointed (Krohmer did the build-out himself) with seating for around 50, and the far wall is dominated by a long L-shaped cocktail bar that looks directly into an open kitchen. That bar may look simple, but it's also significant, with knowlegeable bartenders shaking, stirring, and conjuring cocktails to a fare-thee-well.

Then you notice a large menu board and things start falling in place. Other Mama is an American/Japanese izakaya/sushi/raw bar/gastropub. Got that? Krohmer cut his seafood teeth with Iron Chef Morimoto (in Philadelphia) and honed his skills locally at Sen of Japan, just down the street. He specializes in strong flavors paired with impeccably chosen seafood, such as his oysters foie Rockefeller—a dish that combines sweet and salty bivalves with an umami-bomb of duck liver. Everything from the raw bar—from amberjack crudo with Meyer lemon and scallop carpaccio to a sashimi salad with thyme and honey—competes with anything you'll find 10 miles to the east at two-thirds the price, and his pork-belly kimchee fried rice, seafood toban yaki, and caviar French toast prove Krohmer can pull together proteins and starches in unlikely combinations as well.

Gone are the days when all-you-can-eat sushi bars defined our fish eating off the Strip. Almost overnight, Other Mama upped everyone's game and put to rest the idea that you have to travel to Las Vegas Boulevard South to get the good stuff.

GET THIS

Oysters foie Rockefeller; amberjack crudo; pork-belly kimchee fried rice; Penn Cove mussels. BLT BBQ oysters; octopus ceviche; Jidori chicken thighs; sashimi combination; French toast caviar; Japanese fried chicken; hush puppies blue crab; deviled eggs fried oyster; vegetable tempura; whole grilled fish.

PAMPLONA COCKTAILS & TAPAS (WEST) Spanish

see map 1, page 233
5781 W. Sahara Avenue, #100
(702) 659-5781
pamplonalv.com
Sun., Tues.-Thurs., 3-10 p.m.; Fri.-Sat., 3-11 p.m.
$25-$75

Las Vegas saw three separate tapas restaurants open this past year (in the same area of town) and lovers of tempranillo, pulpo, and patatas bravas couldn't be happier. Pamplona is the most purely Spanish of the bunch and Chef Ariel Zuniga's versions of everything from paella Valenciana to pulpo asado (grilled octopus with chimichurri sauce) are so good, they'll save you a ticket to Madrid.

Occupying a corner of a set-back nondescript strip mall on a stretch of road home to car lots both full and vacant, nothing on the facade gives any warning of how serene and polished an operation this is. A cozy bar serves superb sangria, while the dining room provides the comfort (and real linens) sadly lacking in so many modern restaurants today.

Start your meal with the jamón serrano on crusty bread or the spicy sobrasada-sausage spread. Move on to some Peruano snapper ceviche with piquillo peppers, then buckle your seatbelt for the most authentic versions of aceitunas (olives), patatas bravas (baby potatoes), setas al ajillo (mixed mushrooms with lots of garlic), piquillo relleno de queso de cabra (roasted stuffed peppers), and a

John Curtas

tortilla Español that Las Vegas has ever seen. Not to take anything away from Julian Serrano (the chef or the restaurant) or José Andrés, but once you've tasted these versions, there's no longer any reason to endure the nickel and diming of the Aria or Cosmopolitan hotels to get your bite of Spain.

As you tango through the menu, the hits keep coming: croquetas de pollo as good as anything Jaleo can throw at you and gambas al ajillo that are guaranteed to drive away all vampires. Garlic is to Spanish food what butter is to French, so gird your loins for some of the most pungent dishes you've ever experienced. This isn't to say the dishes are bereft of subtlety (LeBlanc knows how to balance his flavors), but only to give fair warning that sharing is essential unless you want to knock your partner over with your breath later in the evening. They also do a fine job with all of their plancha'd, grilled, and skewered meats here—all aggressively spiced and seasoned— with the honey-glazed pork belly and finger-licking-good lamb chops the ones not to miss.

About the only thing that disappoints is the unimaginative wine list. In this era of so much interesting wine coming out of Spain, Portugal, and South America (at all price points), the bottles do justice to neither the food nor the atmosphere. And even though no one's going to drink it but me, there should be several sherries offered by the glass. Much more thought is given to the beautiful fruit ices and cinnamon-sugar-dusted warm buñuelos; like the rest of the menu, they highlight the balance, intensity, and passion behind Spanish cooking. Lovers of all things Español should take note and make a beeline here.

GET THIS

Jamon serrano; sobrasada sausage; ceviche; aceitunas (olives); patatas bravas (potatoes); setas al ajillo (mixed mushrooms); piquillo peppers; gambas (shrimp); tortilla Español (Spanish potato and egg omelet); pork belly; lamb chops; buñuelos.

see map 1, page 233
3839 Spring Mountain Road
(702) 582-5852
partage.vegas
Mon.-Thurs., 5-10 p.m.; Fri.-Sat., 5-11 p.m.
$75-$125

The chefs are French, the decor is French, the bartenders are French, and the food is as French as Bastille Day. And the whole enchilada is in Chinatown. Go figure.

When Yuri Szarzewski, Vincent Pellerin, and Nicolas Kalpokdjian came to the United States in 2015, they had a dream: They wanted to bring healthy French food to Las Vegas. Anyone with a brain would've told them the idea had as much chance for success as a Mormon nightclub, but arrive and succeed they did, first with their casual EATT Gourmet Bistro on West Sahara and now with a more upscale (but still very laid back) place in a shopping center more at home with massage parlors and noodle shops than croque monsieurs and Pays Nantes.

Partage means "sharing" and the menu encourages you to do just that. Twenty small-plate options are offered, each amounting to no more than two to three bites of headliners like halibut ceviche (disguised to look like dragon fruit) or a perfect meaty scallop swimming in a dashi broth with seaweed chutney and steamed leeks. Everyone seems to feature trilogies of oysters these days and the version here is top drawer, with the yuzu hollandaise being the one that keeps you smiling. As good as they are, the real stars of the show are the salmon croquettes and the squid "risotto"—the risotto in this case being finely diced squid bound together by a barely there pesto, filled with flavor, but not filling you up.

If you're looking for richness, Szarzewski has you covered. His sweetbreads are a godsend for lovers of all things thymus, accented by lotus root and a smooth tonka bean cream; the tight little sautéed bundle of soft white meat hides how dense and filling this offal can be. For pure decadence, though, nothing beats his oxtail croque monsieur: long-simmered meat, slicked with bone marrow, served between three batons of the world's most luxurious toast. Jamón platters are everywhere these days, but this little one may be the cutest of them all.

The anti-ham crowd will enjoy digging into ratatouille-stuffed squash blossoms, a burrata Caprese salad, a melange of root veggies, and the best damn pea soup you've ever slurped.

Large groups will want to go large format with big cuts of 18-ounce rib eye or a 32-ounce tomahawk steak—smoked with either hickory, applewood, or hay (your choice!). Two-pound lobsters, whole duckling breasts served on the bone, and sea bass baked in salt crust are also offered for the whole table to swoon over. In keeping with the "healthy French" thing, sauces are kept to a minimum. Not to my taste, exactly—the duck, pork, and bass suffer from the lack of liquids—but the presentations are in keeping with how modern French food is done these days.

For dessert, Pellerin's rolling cart is not to be missed. Whether he's doing a baba au rhum (injected at table with some high-proof spirit), profiteroles, or a flaming baked Alaska, every one of his classics is hand-tooled and as tasty as anything on the Strip. Pastry chefs are an endangered species these days and it's great to have a local one working his sweet magic in two restaurants. The macarons (when available) should be ordered by the dozen.

GET THIS

Halibut ceviche; oysters; scallop in dashi; lobster ravioli; squid "risotto"; pea soup; pata negra ham; sweetbreads; salmon croquettes; squash blossoms; Caprese salad; smoked tomahawk steak; duck breast; whole fish; macarons; baba au rhum; baked Alaska.

PIZZERIA MONZU [EAST]

Italian

see map 1, page 233
6020 W. Flamingo Road, #10
(702) 749-5959
monzulv.com
Sun.-Wed., 11 a.m.-9:30 p.m.; Thurs.-Sat., 11 a.m.-11 p.m.;
Sun., 11 a.m.-3 p.m.
$25-$75

Las Vegas upped its pizza game considerably over the past decade, but it wasn't until Pizzeria Monzú opened this year that it had a true Sicilian superstar. It's something of an insult that food this good is located right behind an Arby's in a strip mall that's seen better days, but there it is, beckoning like no other Italian in town. Sicilian restaurant scion Giò Mauro (of Nora's family fame) took over the old Nora's (the new one is now a block away) and expanded and modernized it. What was once old-school Italian-American now reeks of wood smoke, craft cocktails, and foodie cred.

The room is big, bright, and airy; the tables are comfortable and well-spaced. High ceilings keep the noise level down to conversational levels and a small stage off to one side gives you a hint that live entertainment will be in the offing. Those wanting upscale spritzers and gorgeous (all-Italian) wines by the glass won't be disappointed and if you're looking for some serious beer and wines by the bottle, you'll sit up and take notice. Twelve brews on draft range from local IPAs to Michigan brown ales and the wine list is a dream come true—dozens of modestly priced vintages from up and down

John Curtas

the Italian peninsula, all with brief pithy descriptions of what you're getting. It might be the best short wine list in all of Vegas.

Once you're seated, get the appetizers, all of them: squash blossoms stuffed with ricotta and mint, ascolane (sausage-stuffed) olives, stuffed chicken wings, agrodolce (sweet and sour) meatballs, and the brightest of all in this galaxy of six stars, the stuffed lemon leaves, which aren't as much stuffed as they're skewered and grilled in leafy envelopes. Each order is enough for four, so a table full of these plates makes a meal unto itself.

If you insist, the salumi and fromaggi antipasti are also good places to start, as Mauro is justifiably proud of his meats and cheeses, and the bruschetta (whether plain or speckled with roasted garlic and anchovies, Sicilian-style) will satisfy as well. The only problem with all of these is if you fill up too fast, you won't have room for the main event: pizza alla pala. As big as a small desk and easily feeding four to six hungry adults, these big boys come in all sorts of combos.

I'm partial to the Simple (crushed tomatoes, basil, and mozzarella), but the Regina Margherita gets a deeper sweetness from cherry tomatoes and a certain tang (from buffalo mozz) that's as far from your average slice as the *Godfather II* is from *Sharknado*. No matter which one you get (though some of the combos like Pork Reigns and Vegas Meets Italy are a tad overloaded for our tastes), you can't help but notice the chewy, tangy, dense, and satisfying bread providing the foundation. This is serious stuff: long fermented dough from an ancient starter that shines on its own. 'Tis almost a pity to cover up this toothsome crumb with bacon, goat cheese, and arugula (Apricot) or gorgonzola, walnuts, and honey ('Nduja), but if you do, you'll still find yourself fighting your tablemates for the last slice.

I'm told that the large proteins offered here—Polpettone (giant meatball), grilled swordfish, and a 34-ounce rib eye Fiorentina—are wonderful, but I'm always too busy grooving on the pizza to notice. The one I've had, Crepe Lasagna, a.k.a. crespelle al forno, was a meaty, cheesy, béchamel delight.

Anyone who doesn't order Sfgini di San Giuseppe (fist-sized Sicilian doughnuts filled with sweetened ricotta) should be consigned to sleep with the fishes.

GET THIS

Ascolane olives; squash blossoms; sweet and sour meatballs; sausage-stuffed lemon leaves; Sicilian garlic bread; salumi and formaggi; Giovanni's salad; pizza alla pala; Sicilian-style doughnuts.

RAKU & SWEETS RAKU (WEST)   Japanese

see map 1, page 233
5030 Spring Mountain Road, #2-#3
(702) 367-3511 / (702) 290-7181
raku-grill.com
Raku: Mon.-Sat., 6 p.m.-2 a.m. / Sweets Raku: Mon.-Tues. & Thurs.-Fri.,
6 p.m.-midnight; Sat., noon-midnight; Sun., noon-9 p.m.
$25-$75

Raku and Sweets Raku aren't simply places to eat; they're statements of quality and passion, a dedication to excellence that can
no longer be faked or phoned in, either on or off the Strip. You can
thank Japanese émigré Mitsuo Endo for this taste revolution (not
some absentee celebrity chef who treats Vegas like an easy-access
ATM machine). The next great meal you have off the Strip, be it a
humble noodle joint or a fancy chef-driven room, owes more than
a little nod to Endo-san's continuing quest for perfection. It was
he who made Spring Mountain Road a foodie destination, lifting it
above its roots as a forlorn stretch of bargain-basement Asian eats.

Japanese izakaya, oden, and robata cooking was virtually unheard
of when Raku opened in early 2008. With only his authentic sensibilities to guide him, Endo has taught Las Vegas just how great Japanese cooking can be. Izakayas are everywhere these days, strutting
their stuff and educating palates like nobody's business, but Raku,
hidden in a corner of a small Spring Mountain Road strip mall, gave
Las Vegas its first taste of binchotan charcoal cooking and pork
cheek, beef silver skin, and tomato with bacon and asparagus, which

John Curtas

are just as stunning today as they were when the place opened. The agedashi tofu and foie gras egg custard are studies in steamed minimalism, and what this tiny kitchen does with oily fish is legendary. There's a fixed menu of all of the above, but true Japronauts wait for the daily-specials chalk board to come around, then just point and enjoy the ride.

Raku is for a certain type of adventuresome food lover, but its sweet sister parked a few doors down serves finely crafted desserts (and small savory bites, and lunch on weekends) that can either be analyzed, admired for their art, or consumed wholesale, depending on your mood. French technique blended with Japanese precision is a match made in heaven and Sweets Raku takes a back seat to no one when it comes to eye-popping sugar creations.

Endo-san may not be aware of the revolution he started, but I am. *Domo arigato* and *gochisousama* ("Thank you for feeding us"), Mitsuo Endo.

GET THIS

Raku: Agedashi tofu; Kobe beef liver sashimi; ayu nanbantsuke (sweet marinated smelt); beef silver skin ebishinjo (shrimp) souffle; kurobuta pork cheek; fried ice fish; sashimi salad; Raku tofu; poached egg with sea urchin and salmon roe; sunomono salad; Tsukune-grilled ground chicken; Kobe beef liver.

Sweets Raku: Les fromages japonaise; foie gras; weekend lunch; Japanese omelet; salmon sandwich; all desserts.

RESTAURANT GUY SAVOY [STRIP]   French

Caesars Palace
(702) 731-7286
caesarspalace.com
Wed.-Sun., 5:30-9:30 p.m.
$125 and up

A meal at Restaurant Guy Savoy is an event. You can feel it as you approach the giant dark doors down the tucked-away hallway and you can sense it as you're led into the cathedral-like space boasting what may be the tallest ceiling in gastronomia. But once you're seated, you'll share the room with only a few other souls.

Economist Tyler Cowen has counseled avoiding any restaurant where "groups of people (especially beautiful women) are laughing loudly and having a good time," indicating people are there for anything but the food. You'll never encounter this at RGS. Here, the tones will be hushed and the reverence palpable. Like its competitor Joël Robuchon down the street, there is a sense of food being cooked, plated, and consumed as part of a secular religion. Robuchon is like a temple of fine dining, while Savoy is more of a chapel (that high-ceiling thing again.) Regardless, the patrons here are very serious about what they eat and drink.

Top toque Nicolas Costagliola now oversees all the classics that made Guy famous—"Peas All Around," "Colors of Caviar," artichoke truffle soup, and Guinea hen au cocotte—but also exotica like

John Curtas

"Santa Barbara spot prawns caught in a sweet-and-sour fishnet" (a blanket of mesh-cut daikons) or wild salmon "cooked" on a slab of dry ice, a conceit brought tableside that turns the fish into a dense toothsomeness unknown to most fish lovers.

French chefs know foie gras like Koreans know cabbage and Asseo and his brigade de cuisine are no slouches in this arena, offering small cubes of horseradish-topped foie over poached celery stalks dressed with "potato-chip bouillon," a dish that tastes exactly like it sounds. Modernist touches are scattered here and there, for example lobster, beets, and crab bathed with "cold steam," but what keeps me coming back are the classics, such as veal three ways and a mosaic of milk-fed poularde and foie gras, circular discs of the finest grained paté you can imagine. In fall, there is the famous pumpkin soup served from the gourd and showered with white truffles. The turbot a la plancha with sea urchin and black rice is a treat no matter what season it is, and the bread and cheese carts are the stuff of which dreams are made.

Accompanying it all is the biggest and best wine list in town—so big it needs its own table and so good you'll be able to find the perfect bottle in the $75-$125 range as easily as a cult Cabernet or a classified growth. Anyone who drinks anything but wine with this food needs to have their head examined.

Restaurants like Guy Savoy, Joël Robuchon, and Twist don't really have any competition in town. These Big Three compete only with one another and themselves. As the only American outposts of three of the most iconic French chefs on Earth, there is preciseness on the plate that few places in the world can match. Savoy's menu may not be as innovative as Gagnaire's or as involved as Robuchon's, but on any night of the week, its ingredients and cooking stand shoulder to shoulder with them.

Las Vegas is lucky to have all three within a mile of one another. I'm lucky that each is only ten minutes from my house.

GET THIS

Marinated grilled hamachi with egg-sherry vinegar; eggplant sherry and radish gelée; mosaic of milk-fed poularde; oysters en gelée; pintade (guinea fowl); Peas All Around, truffle-artichoke soup; Colors of Caviar; turbot a la plancha; lobster and lump crab in cold steam; salmon "iceberg"; veal three ways; bread and cheese, then more bread and more cheese; wine.

The 52 Essential

ROOSTER BOY CAFE (WEST) American

see map 2, page 234
2620 Regatta Drive, #113
(702) 560-2453
roosterboycafe.com
Tue.-Sun., 7:30 a.m.-3 p.m.
$25 or less

Good restaurants start with good groceries and chef/owner Sonia El-Nawal is justifiably proud of hers. If there's a more locavore, personal, handmade restaurant in town, I haven't found it. Rooster Boy is every food-lover's dream: a tiny restaurant where the chef is at the stoves every day, sourcing local ingredients and cooking and baking her heart out. This type of intimate place nurtures the soul of a food community and Las Vegas still has too few of them.

Having worked with industry giants Jean-Georges Vongerichten and Julian Serrano, El-Nawal's résumé has taken her to San Francisco, the Big Apple, Miami, and finally Las Vegas. Along the way, she's invented desserts for Nobu, boiled bagels in Brussels, and catered in Mexico City. Her presence here might be the equivalent of Meryl Streep doing community theater, but we're lucky to have an all-star slumming it in our midst.

The cozy dining alcove (practically hidden from the parking lot) has tables laden with pastries and the vibe tells you whatever you get will be top-notch. Watching the chef/owner patrol the premises and work the line confirms the point.

John Curtas

Much is made of El-Nawal's Rooster Boy Granolas, but for our dinero, your breakfast cravings will be better served by one of her hand-crafted galettes, pastries, or pancakes. And if you skip the Dutch Oven soufflé, then see it go past your table, you'll be immediately gripped by what the Germans call *der futterneid* (food jealousy).

Veggies are market-driven, so you'll get whatever looks good that day—if you're lucky, fresh corn tossed with green onions and walloped with a dollop of creme fraiche and caviar. For something lighter, the From Back Home brings Middle Eastern healthiness in the form of house-baked pillow-y flatbread surrounded by labne, cukes, tomato, and a dusting of zataar.

That same pita provides a foundation for shashouka, eggs poached in a spicy tomato sauce, while El-Nawal's brioche is the starch around the Frenchy, a superlative baked egg unfortunately dressed with white truffle oil. (Don't get me started about chefs' use of "truffle oil.") They also cure wild salmon into a gorgeous gravlax. Try finding another breakfast spot anywhere in Vegas that does this.

All of these are worthy contenders for top menu honors (as are the croissants, ginger cake, and pain au chocolat), but the Mi Corazon chilaquiles deserve special recognition. In place of mamacita's forlorn tortilla chips drenched in sauce and topped with an indifferent egg, here you find fresh-fried crisps laced with cotija cheese, avocado, tomato, and onion, all sitting in a pool of tangy, herbaceous, green-chile sauce. The peppery bite is there, but also something deeper, more elemental, more ingredient-driven—exactly what you'd expect when a cultural standard gets refracted through the lens of a top chef.

Rooster Boy serves excellent La Colombe coffee, and espresso. You pour your own if all you want is a cup of Joe, but the fancier cortados, cappuccinos, and con leches are just as compelling.

On weekends, the lines form early, so first-timers should go midweek, when it's just Sonia, her tiny staff, and a few regulars at the counter or outdoor tables. What they accomplish in a restaurant of less than 500 feet square is something you need to see for yourself.

GET THIS

Chilaquiles; Shakshouka eggs; Frenchy, baked egg in brioche; croissant; pain au chocolat; ginger cake; granola; breakfast galette; wild salmon gravlax; Dutch Oven/buttermilk pancake; From Back Home labne with pita; coffee.

SAGE (STRIP)

American/French

Aria at CityCenter
(702) 590-8690
aria.com
Sun.-Tues. & Fri., 6-10 p.m.;
Sat., 6-10:30 p.m.
$75-$125

If Sage were in any other foodie capital in America (including such bastions of snobbery like New York and San Francisco), it would be considered one of the best restaurants in town. If it were in Portland, Austin, or Pittsburgh, it would be considered the best restaurant in town. If it weren't located in a huge Las Vegas hotel, it would've won a James Beard Award by now, and if frogs had wings, they wouldn't thump their asses against the ground. Shed no tears for Shawn McClain, however, because he's content to run what is, along with Guy Savoy, a cathedral of fine food that demands precise attention to the catechisms occurring on the plate. If you've ever wondered about the best way to roast a carrot, brûlée some foie gras, grill some octopus, or serve lamb belly with romesco, merguez sausage, and pomegranate, they've got the answers.

The first thing you notice about Sage is how tall it is. Its 20-foot façade and ceilings announce some serious intentions. Likewise, the long bar—backed by a wall of serious spirits, including a fabulous selection of bourbons—is so sleek and welcoming that it makes me wish I were an alcoholic. You'll be tempted to park yourself at a stool and let the bartenders dazzle you with their footwork. Also tempting is the bar menu itself: something of a microcosm of the main room, showing off this kitchen's facility with oysters, eggs, scallops, and hanger steak. You could just nibble and sip there and die happy, but then you'd miss out on the dramatic main room where the fun really begins.

I'm not usually a fan of tasting menus; they're always too long, showoffy, and dictatorial ("You vil eet zee veal bladder wit chocolate soos and you vil like eet!"). But here they do it right. Six savory courses are offered, all sized for enjoyment and concocted with genius. Ora king salmon gets the right amount of shock from lemon, dill, and horseradish, warm corn custard comes with langoustines and chorizo, and a loin of spring lamb gets a crispy lamb-neck garnish. The sauces are always superb (vin jaune on organic chicken, miso soubise on skirt steak, béarnaise on beef) and the salads are so artistic, you won't want to disturb them. Sweetbreads don't show up enough in restaurants for our taste, but here they're roasted reverentially (to juicy and still fork-tender) and served on white polenta with glazed bacon. A more satisfying thymus gland you will never encounter.

It's a testament to the excellence of Las Vegas restaurants that Sage is considered just another slugger in a lineup of great places to have dinner. It's not cheap, but it's so tasty you won't mind getting converted to the cult of Shawn McClain.

GET THIS

Bourbon; kusshi oysters with tequila mignonette; oxtail crostini; foie gras crème brûlée; hanger steak; roasted carrots; heirloom tomato salad; Hamachi crudo salad; ora king salmon; loin of spring lamb; veal cheeks; corn custard with langoustines; lamb belly; organic chicken with sauce vin jaune; roasted sweetbreads; slow-poached farm egg; whatever they're whipping up for dessert.

Bellagio
(702) 693-8181
wolfgangpuck.com/dining/spago-lv
Sun.-Thurs., 11:30 a.m.-10:30 p.m.; Fri. & Sat., 11:30 a.m.-11 p.m.
$25-$75

No matter what Spago does, it does well. No matter what you order, expect it to be one of the best versions you've ever had. Call it Wolfgang Puck magic; call it great management; call it hiring good chefs at the top of their game. Whatever it is, one thing sets Spago apart from its competitors—an almost military precision to its food.

Las Vegas got its first taste of Spago in December 1992, and for the next 25 years, it loomed large over the Strip dining scene as the granddaddy of our great restaurants. When its lease was finally up at the Forum Shops in 2018, it decamped for Bellagio to take over the old Olives space and got a bright modern makeover into Spago 2.0. The bar still hugs the right side of the restaurant and low-slung table seating allows you to eat or linger near all those top-shelf cocktails. Large windows and glass doors now frame an outdoor patio that provides excellent seating for the fountain show. (The many outdoor tables go fast, so reserve ahead for *al fresco*.)

Whether you sit outdoors or in, the menu provides the soothing satisfaction Puck has always delivered: a blend of classics, such as veal wiener schnitzel, steamed cod Hong Kong-style, smoked

John Curtas

salmon pizzas, and crispy-skin branzino; the seasonal, like sweet-corn agnolotti, heirloom-tomato salad, Santa Barbara spot prawns, and vegetable ragout; and the formidable—veal chop, lamb rack, and a côte de bouef for two.

Whatever specials your waiter recites, from big-eye tuna crudo to foie gras ice cream, rest assured they'll be worth the tariff.

Mark Andelbradt, a Puck veteran, has been at the helm since the move to the new digs and his facility with pasta is every bit as nimble as his command of roasted cauliflower. If his proteins are the equal of a steakhouse, his noodles match up against any Italian. More than once, I've done a side-by-side comparison of Spago's housemade pastas with some celeb-chef versions around town and every time Spago's has come out on top. Andelbradt's spicy lamb Bolognese cavatelli, squid-ink garganelli, and those agnolotti are textbook examples of these standards and when he's doing saffron-seafood risotto, don't miss it.

When you're done with the savories, the sweets are waiting to destroy your willpower. The spiked-lemon-with-yuzu cream chiffon cake and citrus mousse has been on the menu so long, it's almost as iconic as those pizzas. The baked-to-order chocolate-chip cookies are worth a trip by themselves, but the thing to get is Wolfgang's Kaiserschmarren, a showstopping souffléd pancake for two that actually feeds four.

Though the bar is a great place to catch a game, the wine list holds few surprises. (It was pretty boring at the old location too.) Stick with the by-the-glass selections.

All of America owes a debt to Spago for the way we eat nowadays. Open kitchens, upgraded pizzas, casual dining with killer food—they all started with Spago. In a way, every gastropub from Portland, Maine, to Portland, Oregon, is an homage to the type of cooking first popularized by Wolfgang Puck. But he did it first and in many ways, Spago still does it best.

GET THIS

Artisanal salumi pizza; smoked-salmon pizza; spicy-shrimp pizza; tuna tartare; Gulf shrimp cocktail; prime beef burger; field-mushroom soup; roasted cauliflower; veal wiener schnitzel; steamed cod; branzino; all pastas; seafood-saffron risotto; vegetable ragout; veal chop; lamb rack; côte de boeuf rib eye for two; foie gras ice cream; cookie platter; spiked lemon with yuzu cream; Kaiserschmarren.

SPARROW + WOLF (WEST)

American

see map 1, page 233
4480 Spring Mountain Road, #100
(702) 790 2147
sparrowandwolflv.com
5-11 p.m., daily
$25-$75

Sparrow + Wolf is sleek and small (60 seats) and smells of wood smoke—all indicia of the haute-eclectic-bistro cooking that has taken over America in the past decade. Gastronomades who wander the Earth in search of oases of ingenious edibles have already pitched their tents here. Intrepid gastronauts, addicted to traveling where no man has gone before, have been here since day one. Simple gastronomes who revel in chef-enhanced high-quality ingredients will not be disappointed, either. But if you're the type who finds Spring Mountain Road too challenging (both geographically and gastronomically) or if you're simply looking for a good plate of grub, the sledding might be a tad heavy.

This is not to damn the culinary musings of Chef Brian Howard with faint praise, but only to point out that there's a lot going on here, both in your glass and on your plate. "Simple" is not a word in Howard's vocabulary. With this long-awaited opening in the heart of Chinatown, he threw down a gauntlet among the pho parlors and noodle shops and immediately complicated non-Asians' relationship to this three-mile-long pan-Pacific island of culinary delights.

John Curtas

Just as complicated are the cocktails—at least five ingredients each—but they're as tasty as the food if you go for that sort of thing. The wine list matches the menu, the neighborhood, and the crowd, even if it doesn't match what a wine snob might want to drink.

Howard's good eats begin with his charcuterie platter: not yet made in-house, but top-quality stuff. Alongside these meats are seasonal pickles he does make on the premises and they're fabulous. Just as good are his oysters topped three different ways, with pineapple mignonette, cucumber granité, and a yuzu pearl. The Chinatown clams casino, baked with uni (sea urchin) hollandaise, is so rich it ought to come with its own calorie count, but it's also fusion food at its finest.

Like I said, nothing is simple; roasted beets come under a tangle of endive, pea shoots, shaved fennel, sheep's-milk blue cheese, and "bird seed" (black sesame seeds)! Quite a mouthful, but everything has its place. Butcher Wings with burnt-tomato 'nduja vinaigrette are one in a bevy of beautiful plates that dot the menu: beef-cheek with bone-marrow dumplings, sweetbreads with smoked bacon, firm toothsome halibut coated with Alabama white-barbecue sauce, and udon noodles "Bolognese" with Taggiasche olives, citrus confit, and mint. Octopus on top of a very good steak sounds contrived, but if you taste carefully and think a little harder, you see that a lot of consideration went into these combinations, and by and large they work. Nowhere is this payoff more rewarding than in his Campfire Duck, gorgeous slices of duck and foie gras resting on dark earthy shreds of wood-ear mushrooms, accented by sharp bites of salted plum in a duck-bone broth. It's a dish that appears to be trying to do too much, but those flavor explosions in your mouth tell you that it succeeds.

This is high-wire cooking without a net, and when Howard pulls it off, the results are thrilling indeed.

GET THIS

House-baked bread; oysters three ways; halibut with white Alabama BBQ sauce; Campfire Duck; Butcher Wings; Chinatown clams casino; udon "Bolognese"; beef-cheek and bone-marrow dumplings; charcuterie; sweetbreads with smoked bacon.

TATSUJIN X (WEST) Japanese

see map 1, page 233
4439 W. Flamingo Road
(702) 771-8955
Mon.-Sat., 6 p.m.-2 a.m.
$75-$125

This unique Japanese restaurant is a fixed-price fixed-meal steak-house (with some à la carte options). It's the closest you can get to Tokyo without flying there.

You pay one price ($50-$70) and receive eight dishes, four of which give you some choice (salad, protein, pancake or rice, and dessert). In Asia, these fixed-price "sets" aren't for picky eaters, nor for those who demand to know whether they'll "like something" before they order it. The whole idea behind teppanyaki restaurants is to sit down, enjoy the show, and let the chefs work their magic.

The showier aspects of this food gave rise to the post-WW II Jap-anese-steakhouse craze, with thrown knives and flamed food, all to the oohs and ahhs of prom dates everywhere. But crowd-pleasing this place is not. If Benihana is a steakhouse show for the masses, Tatsujin X is a private concert by a virtuoso.

In the middle of an old strip mall near the Palms, Tatsujin ("Mas-ter") is the most recent addition to our expanding catalogue of authentic Asian eats and might be the last word in nondescript eat-eries. As in Japan, the signage tells you nothing but the name.

Those in the know will discern its name to denote the teppanyaki

John Curtas

cooking of Japan: the flat steel griddle (teppan) on which various foodstuffs are grilled, broiled, or pan-fried (yaki). Call it a teppan, plancha, or good old frying pan, it's a hot smooth metal surface upon which these dexterous chefs work wonders. What Grand Chef Yoshinori Nakazawa aims for at this spare 13-seat counter isn't the applause of teenagers or tourists, but the sort of gratitude bestowed by black-belt epicureans who know the right stuff when they taste it—an eight-course meal like nothing in Vegas.

A platter of crispy sawagani crab flanked by bright salmon tartare, spicy edamame beans, and meltingly tender strips of barely grilled rib eye sets you up for the well-paced courses to come, from a sparkling wakame salad to a dashimaki-tamago omelet wrapped around strands of king crab and sea urchin. If this town has a bigger umami-bomb than this egg concoction, I've yet to find it.

As you're swooning from the seafood omelet, you'll notice the seafood star of the show: a ginormous oyster the size of a filet mignon. From there you'll move on to simple teppan-grilled vegetables that act as an intermezzo to the proteins: three steaks (filet, rib eye, strip) with a fourth of imported Japanese Wagyu (for a $35 surcharge). Sea bass (excellent) and salmon (good) are a bone thrown to non-meat eaters, but they sort of miss the point of the joint. The steaks are the stars here and they're lightly seasoned and gently cooked as perfectly as beef can be. There's no denying the melt-in-your-mouth appeal of the expensive Wagyu, but my Japanese friends profess to like the denser beefy quality of the American "Kobe" better. Either way, the cuts are seared to a level of succulence you don't achieve with the pyrotechnics of charcoal grilling.

For the final savory course, choose either a thick pork-filled okonomi-yaki pancake or garlic rice. The pancake, served with waving katsuobushi (bonito) flakes, would almost be a meal in itself somewhere else and the garlic rice is a testament to great food coming in deceptively simple packages. This is a grown-up rice dish for connoisseurs of starch.

The three desserts are very Japanese. If you're very Japanese, you'll love them. If not, stick to the ice cream.

GET THIS

Steak set; Japanese Wagyu; American "Kobe" rib eye; sea bass; à la carte items: marinated vegetables; Tatsujin rice; grilled salmon; baked oyster; house-made tofu

THE BLACK SHEEP (WEST)

Asian Fusion

see map 2, page 234
8680 W. Warm Springs Road
(702) 954-3998
blacksheepvegas.com
5-10 p.m., daily; Brunch: Sun., 11 a.m.-2 p.m.
$25-$75

Jamie Tran is no bigger than a *goi cuon* (spring roll) and her restaurant is only 50 seats. But together, these pocket dynamos are pioneering neighborhood dining in a big way.

The Black Sheep's modest dimensions belie its ambitions. Within you'll find a small bar toward the back and a loyal following of local foodies who have turned this unassuming storefront into a mecca for a unique blend of Asian-meets-American.

Calling her food all over the map is an understatement. But this is one time the term "fusion food" fits. Tran turns salmon skins into tacos, perfumes duck confit with lemongrass, and punctuates Indonesian corn fritters with mango salsa. There's not a metaphor she doesn't mix, but after a bite or two, you'll be calling it spot-on delicious in a "I never thought of that" way.

Dishes as diverse as duck prosciutto salad, Thai basil shrimp ceviche, and "hot chicken" on honey toast come at you from multiple directions, but once in the mouth, they make sense. Tran is playing with her food, but she's equally at home sautéing vegan Vietnamese noodles, deep-frying a whole trout, and braising a lamb belly …

John Curtas

after spicing very French flageolet with the scents of Vietnam.

Then there's brunch—a meal most of us epicureans love to hate. The most confusing of meals (booze for breakfast? dessert for lunch?) is usually caloric and boring beyond words. Somehow, in the Tran oeuvre, it achieves angles that will keep you fascinated.

The old reliables like challah French toast and chicken and waffles quickly announce themselves as anything but standards. The eggy toast gets a brandy syrup bath, eggs Benedict lie over meltingly rich soft ropes of lemongrass short ribs, and Tran's hot chicken goes full kaarage, managing a sweethotcrunch from chicken set off by mustard seeds, fermented cabbage, and sriracha. You can also go with traditional steak and eggs here (Creekstone Farms beef topped with a fried egg), a perfect soufflé pancake, or watch Tran indulge her heritage with deep-fried Vietnamese Imperial rolls, given a boost with better ingredients (Duroc pork, briny shrimp) than you'll ever find in a same-old same-old pho parlor.

If the menu has a signature dish, it's the hot chicken, but the crackling Imperial rolls and bao sliders—with housemade pork sausage—give it a run for your money. The sausage gets its kick from fish sauce and the sliders cover all the flavor bases with their adornment of oozing quail egg, crispy shallots, and jalapeño-spiked aioli.

Bargain-hunting oenophiles know the wine list is the real libation star, where Veuve Cliquot champagne sells for $95 and Gaja Promis for $90, marked up at double the wholesale price, not triple the retail like they do on the Strip. By-the-glass offerings all hover around $10 and there's even a selection of funky amaros.

The Black Sheep calls itself a "New American Kitchen," but it's not like any American kitchen you've ever been in, or Vietnamese, for that matter. It's American food filtered through an Asian American at home blending the two cultures on a plate. In doing so, Jamie Tran is paying homage to both cuisines and pioneering a new vocabulary of restaurant food. It's much more revolutionary than people realize. It's the direction in which all American food is headed.

GET THIS

Salmon skin tacos; steak tartare; fried beef crisps; Imperial rolls; bao sliders; fried whole rainbow trout; lemongrass duck confit; braised short rib; brunch; scallion and soufflé pancakes; challah French toast; housemade pork sausage; tres leches cake; macarons; cheesecake; persimmon bread pudding.

THE KITCHEN AT ATOMIC (DOWNTOWN)   American

see map 1, page 233
927 Fremont Street
(702) 534-3223
kitchenatatomic.vegas
Sun., Wed., & Thurs., 5 p.m.-midnight; Fri.-Sat., 5 p.m.-2 a.m.;
Brunch: Sat.-Sun., 10 a.m.-2:30 p.m.
$25-$75

The Kitchen at Atomic resides in the shiny renovated space adjacent to the popular Atomic Liquors bar. In a previous life, it was a gas station. In its present incarnation, it strikes you as a sleek and somewhat cold industrial space no more than 50 feet from its louche neighbor next door. The incongruity lies with these two conjoined siblings existing in two separate universes. At AL, you drink; at TKAA, the food is the star. And quite a star it is, even if the beer and cocktail-swilling hordes next door don't know it.

The menu checks all the right boxes as a destination restaurant—highly vetted veggies, cured fish, charcuterie platter, artisanal greens, appetizers hinting at the kitchen's creativity and mains driving the point home. The attention to detail given to grilled long beans (dappled with feta) or a cold cucumber/grape gazpacho announces a new level of cooking for downtown and offering a whole fish at market price is a bold move for a neighborhood still pockmarked with vacant lots and tattoo parlors.

Glistening knobs of quivering marrow may be as foreign to East Fremont Street as a hooker with teeth, but you'll forget where you

John Curtas

are as you slather these jewels of adipose protein on the nutty toasted bread served with them. Grilled halloumi cheese might not fit with the neighborhood either, but the squeaky fromage will fit just fine as an appetizer for four. Raw seafood is everywhere these days, but the Hamachi crudo, or denser cured striped bass (not the usual tedious fluke), are both light and punch-packing either with chili lime or sumac-and-sherry vinegar. The grilled clams (crusted with chili-flecked bread crumbs) are in a class by themselves. You won't find a better version on or off the Strip.

In many a gastropub, the larger the format, the worse the food gets: big proteins lacking the sexiness of high-concept tweezer food to some chefs. Not so to Executive Chef Jackson Stamper, who seems to lavish just as much attention on pan-seared cauliflower steak and grilled swordfish as he does on his starters. The biggest of his big boys is the Creekstone Farms dry-aged rib eye. It's priced by the ounce and around $80 will get you enough mineral-tinged properly stored steer to feed four. It might not have the mineral tang and Roquefort-like zing of super-aged beef, but you won't find a better steak within three miles of this one.

And then there's the rum-brined chop, a dulcet compaction of pork so luscious and savory you'll re-think your prejudices against this usually boring entrée. Broccoli rabe, rum jus, and mustard seeds complete the picture and you'll be wondering if you've ever had a better one as soon as you finish.

Desserts are more elemental and less chef-y than the savories. The deconstructed apple pie is a nice twist on an old standard and the Guinness chocolate cake (really more like a dense lacquered brownie) will have you reflexively polishing it off in defiance of all your common dieting sense.

They seem to have dialed back the beer and wine list, but it's still interesting and well-priced, probably not enough for a true oenophile, but certainly for the youthful clientele. I won't bother praising the top-shelf cocktails, because a bad mixed drink in Las Vegas is now harder to find than a good mixed drink used to be.

GET THIS

Spring pea salad; grilled long beans; cucumber/grape gazpacho; Hamachi crudo; cured striped bass; bone marrow; grilled Halloumi cheese; charcuterie board; bone-in rib eye; cauliflower steak; porterhouse pork chop; swordfish; apple pie; Guinness chocolate cake.

TWIST BY PIERRE GAGNAIRE French

Waldorf Astoria
(702) 590-8888
waldorfastorialasvegas.com
Tues.-Thurs., 5:30-9:30 p.m.;
Fri.-Sat., 6-10 p.m.
$125 and up

Like a few other restaurants in our Essential 52, Twist isn't for everyone. Like all restaurants in the Pierre Gagnaire oeuvre, it takes a decidedly adventuresome tack toward most of its menu, which consists mainly of riffs on ingredients presented in a blizzard of small plates. If you're looking for portion size or a standard three-course (app-main-dessert) dinner, look elsewhere. But if you're an intrepid epicure, you'll think you've died and gone to heaven. Which pretty much also describes the room, as heavenly and romantic a space (overlooking Aria and the Crystals Mall) as you'll find on the Strip.

Once you're seated, though, the fun really starts. It's impossible to get bored by Gagnaire's food. The menu changes seasonally and very few "standards" are on it, so whatever I rave about—be it shellfish mariniere with champagne herb sauce and black gnocchi or a trio of savory ice creams—might be long gone by the time you show up. Take heart. This former enfant terrible of French cuisine will capture your attention from the first array of amuse bouche through flights of oyster fancy, accented with everything from sardine rillettes and blue curaçao to frozen bananas. How does he think these things up? Who knows, but they invariably work and keep you smiling and guessing throughout the meal.

If you're saddled with a beef 'n' taters dining companion, don't despair. The steaks here are pricey, but meltingly tender and some of the best in town. Does anyone on Earth make better veal tender-

John Curtas

loin? Probably not. Ditto the Bordelaise and Béarnaise sauces. An avant-garde restaurant that also serves tremendous beef (and some of the most stunning vegetarian creations on the planet) sounds like an impossible balancing act, but the chefs here pull off this magic nightly with the consistency of stone masons. The wine list is smaller than those at other top-notch frog ponds, with lots of bottles that won't have you reaching for your heart medicine. When Twist opened in 2009, the wine list was one of the weaker things about it. These days it competes with any (wine) watering hole in town.

Things have gotten a bit more expensive here over the years, but the tasting menus are priced competitively with the likes of Le Cirque ($135-$180), rather than stratospherically like Savoy and Robuchon ($250-$450). Where its competitors feel more like churches of fine dining, Twist is where you go to have fun. French food conquered the world because of the discipline and deliciousness of its recipes. Twist conquered Las Vegas with a blend of perfection and whimsy. On any night of any season, I'll put a meal here up against any in the country.

GET THIS

Vegetarian tasting menu; Grand tasting menu; Pierre's salad; veal tenderloin; Zezette bouillon; Hudson Valley foie gras two ways; smoked haddock and scallop soufflé; Dover sole; wild European turbot; Maine lobster; Nebraska prime rib eye; Pierre's dessert medley.

VETRI CUCINA [WEST] Italian

Palms
(702) 944-5900
palms.com
Sun.-Thurs., 6 p.m.-10 p.m.; Fri.-Sat., 6-11 p.m.
$75-$125

Even at its most basic level, Italian food is soothing. Average Italian food satisfies the way pop music does: It's catchy and forgettable. Great Italian food, like great opera, will take your breath away. Vetri will take your breath away—if you let it.

The qualifier is important. Splendid as it is, Vetri isn't for everyone. There are no easy answers here; crowd-pleasing isn't in its vocabulary. Clichés of all kinds have been shelved. Pizzas are kaput. Soups and scampi have been scuttled. Meatballs are missing in action. Place settings are spartan. Caesar is nowhere to be found. No giant hunks of cheese or curled ribbons of prosciutto are brought to your table. The bread basket is modest and something-for-everyone proteins (pork chops, salmon, chicken breasts) are non-existent.

In other words, if you're looking for typical Italian at a by-the-numbers Italian restaurant, you've come to the wrong place. But if you have the chops for a modern Italian experience—like the best ristorantes in Italy are putting forth these days—you'll think you've died and gone to Bergamo.

All of it is served in a nonpareil setting, 56 floors up, overlooking

John Curtas

the Strip. It's a location that puts the lie to the old adage about the higher off the ground you get, the worse the food is.

Your dinner here should start with foie gras pastrami with brioche and mostarda. From there, proceed to emerald-green Swiss-chard gnocchi with brown butter, tonnarelli grano arso (toasted wheat pasta with seafood), and dark slightly gamy slices of roasted baby goat. For something lighter, dive into a squid and artichoke galette, raw fish crudo, or pickled veggie/antipasti platter, followed by simple spaghetti swirled with chunky San Marzano tomatoes and basil.

In the mood to dance with the big boys? Take down a compacted disc of veal tartare garnished with crisp sweetbreads, a sweet onion crepe (more like a thick, sweet-savory, puck-sized tart) served with white truffle fondue, followed by either a whole roasted branzino or a brontosaurian bistecca Fiorentina (also for two).

Mere plebes will be happy with a gorgeous stuffed guinea-hen breast, thinly sliced porchetta with tuna sauce, casoncellil alla bergamasca (Lombardy's crinkled version of ravioli), and the cutest little bone-marrow raviolini you've ever seen.

The breads are baked in-house, with artisanal wheat (from Arizona, of all places) ground into flour on the premises. You can craft an ideal meal here without ever venturing into the second section and don't be afraid to do so: These pastas are some of the most interesting you'll ever have and the wait staff is happy to help you construct a meal long on creative veggies and unique noodles, though short on big proteins.

Before you get to all these incredible eats, a stop at the bar to take in the view (and grab a cocktail) is mandatory. After that, the wine list isn't exactly chock full of bargains, but at least the prices don't match the altitude—plenty of drinkable stuff mere mortals can afford. The by-the-glass list is a treat and covers the Italian peninsula from Sicily to Tuscany, from the Piemonte to the Veneto. Desserts are ever-changing and always wonderful.

GET THIS

Foie gras pastrami; pickled vegetable/antipasti platter; Swiss chard gnocchi; tonnarelli grano arso; veal tartare with sweetbreads; porchetta with tuna sauce; sweet onion crepe; casoncelli alla begamasca; bone marrow raviolini; whole roasted branzino; roasted baby goat; stuffed Guinea hen; bistecca Fiorentina; bread; dessert.

WEERA THAI KITCHEN (WEST)

Thai

see map 1, page 233
4276 Spring Moutain Road. #105
(702) 485-1688
weerathai.com
11 a.m.-2 a.m., daily
$25-$75

The first thing you'll notice about Weera Thai Kitchen is the décor, quite the upgrade from its homey older sibling on W. Sahara. Oversized flower murals dominate a brightly lit room outfitted with well-spaced modern tables. It immediately signals that you're no longer in copycat Thai-menu land. With the move to Chinatown, Weera Thai's Thonguthaisiri clan is broadcasting its intent to compete with the big boys and join the black-belt foodie club Spring Mountain Road now represents.

When the eye-popping picture menu appears, you'll wonder if all these fascinating dishes taste as good as they look. They do. The only problem you'll have is trying to rein in your eyes as they grow bigger than your stomach with every turn of the page.

Top billing is given to such jaw-droppers as khao yum (blue-tinted butterfly pea rice with toasted coconut), khoa kluk kapi (another rice dish given special pungency by fermented shrimp paste and depth from chunks of pork belly), and goong maenam pao (giant river prawns) or those same prawns with mozzarella, apparently a thing in Thailand. As big as small lobster tails, they're perfect as an appe-

John Curtas

tizer for four or a meal for two.

WTK distinguishes itself from the original restaurant with its emphasis on seafood and lots of spicy street food. Beautiful shrimp wrapped in thin rice noodles are deep-fried in kung sarong, while something called yum hi-so sees slightly slimy raw blue crab get lit up with chili and lime; the spicy squid salad will also give you all the heat you can handle. Seek solace, if you will, in the garlic shrimp, so loaded with melted slices and crispy chips of the stuff you'll think you've died and gone to Allium heaven.

A platter of ma haw or ma hor (literally, galloping horses) might catch your eye. These balls of caramelized minced pork served on pineapple slices are best described as meat candy. Though very sweet, they somehow beckon bite after each teeth-aching bite. If nothing else, the sweet meat sets up your palate for the barrage of penetrating flavors to come.

One of the tamer dishes is ka pow gai kai dao, four bowls containing minced basil chicken, rice, onion, and peppers, and a fried egg, all ready to mix into a one-dish meal, but we'd rather spend our time with sai oua (stuffed-intestine) northern Thai sour sausage or the nam khao tod (crispy rice with sausage), both right up there with Lotus of Siam's for texture and intensity.

They also do a nice dry version of yen ta fo noodle soup, which is much more palatable in the Vegas heat than the same ingredients served in a giant steaming bowl of tomato-laced broth, and you shouldn't miss definitive pad see ewe pong, broad flat noodles with top-shelf shrimp in yellow curry.

You won't find any fault with the pinkish pad kee mow with chicken, but beware the whole pompano lard prik, which poses a bit of a challenge for those used to eating neat little fileted fish.

Dipping sauces are to Thai cuisine what melted butter is to French and these house-made beauties tailored to the main dish always seem to hit the right balance of tart, sweet, herbaceous, and hot. And balance—of food, décor, spice, and service—is what this kitchen is all about.

GET THIS

Yum hi-so; yen ta fo hang; jumbo river prawns; khao yum; ka pow gai-kai dao; sai oui sausage; kung sarong; beef salad; spicy squid salad; papaya salad; garlic shrimp; pad see ewe.

The 52 Essential

WING LEI [STRIP]   Chinese

Wynn Las Vegas
(702) 770-3388
wynnlasvegas.com
Sun.-Thurs., 5:30-9:30 p.m.; Fri.-Sat., 5:30-10 p.m.
$75-$125

Confucius said a man cannot be too careful about what he eats, but he obviously never came to Wing Lei—a place where you can just close your eyes and point and still be assured of eating the best Chinese food east of Shanghai. Not only is it our most elegant Chinese restaurant, but it's also one of the most elegant restaurants in all of Las Vegas, period.

From the smooth-as-Shantung-silk white-glove service and the best Peking duck in the business to garlic beef tenderloin of uncompromising tenderness, this is cuisine fit for a mandarin, especially those who like a little posh and circumstance with their Sichuan prawns. Lest you be someone who complains about paying premium prices for shrimp and stir-fries, keep in mind that the Chinese invented the whole shared-plates thing a couple of millennia ago—they just called it family-style—and it's the perfect way to keep portion and check sizes down.

And remember: These dishes are made with first-class groceries (unlike many a run-of-the-mill Chinese restaurant). Executive Chef Ming Yu doesn't know how to put out anything but an exquisite

John Curtas

plate of food, and his touch with Cantonese and Szechuan spicing is as graceful as the service. I'm not one for superlatives when it comes to steamed fish, but Yu's light touch with everything that swims takes me straight back to Hong Kong. High rollers from Asia (and we get lots of them) demand perfection in their stir-fries, nutty fried rice, and crispy General Tso's chicken, and Yu delivers it in spades. If you're a fan of any classic Chinese dish, from hand-pulled noodles to kung pao chicken, you'll feel like you're tasting these things the way they were meant to be made, not a version you're settling for in some past-its-prime Chinese dive.

There's nothing past its prime about the wine list, which is stocked with the usual big-hitter bottles for big-ego showoffs. The good news is the (relative) bargains to be found therein and the lower-priced nuggets are the ones that go perfectly with this food. Just look for anything German or Alsatian white, or ask the friendly somms for help.

As for desserts, they give lie to my usual advice about sweets in an Asian restaurant: If you want a good dessert in an Asian restaurant, go to a French one. No offense to Confucius, but the dude really could've learned something from diving into some sesame crème brûlée or a kalamansi cheesecake.

GET THIS

Peking duck; General Tso's chicken; steamed fish; garlic beef; seafood hot & sour soup; Alaskan geoduck clam; Dungeness crab (in season); Santa Barbara prawns; wok-tossed scallops; sampan prawns; mu shu pork; napa cabbage with Iberico ham; Yang Chow fried rice; desserts.

YUI EDOMAE SUSHI (WEST)   Japanese

see map 1, page 233
3460 Arville Street, #HS
(702) 202-2408
yuisushi.com
Mon.-Sat., 6-10:30 p.m.
$75-$125

Yui is obscure in location and impossible to see from the street –
both of which lend just the right amount of Edomae (Tokyo-style)
mystery to your experience. Don't be intimidated, though. If you're
open to eating sushi the real way, which is to say the Japanese way,
you will have the greatest raw-fish-eating experience in Las Vegas,
and probably the best Wagyu beef-eating one as well.

Once you secure a reservation (definitely call ahead), you'll be
greeted by the gracious and beautiful Tomoko-san, who will lead
you past a sliding screen door into the land of serene sushi and
sashimi so good, you'll think you're tasting these pristine fish for
the first time. Just as terrific is the true, birth-certified, Japanese A-5
Wagyu, delicately grilled over white smokeless charcoal. No one
puts a finer point on these things than the Land of the Rising Sun,
and the nuances of flavor and texture can sometimes be subtle to
the point of invisibility. But like all things exquisite, if you take the
time to learn about them, you will be richly rewarded.

Where you'll reap these rewards will either be at the eight-seat

John Curtas

sushi bar or one of the three booths facing the chefs (led by chef/ owner Gen Mizoguchi, the sushi master who put Kabuto on the map) as they work. Only two menus are offered: a nigiri tasting consisting of five courses (including 10 individual pieces of sushi) for $68, and an omakase ("chef's choice") menu for $120. The latter gets you those same 10 pieces of careful selected and sliced sushi (all of it sitting atop slightly warmed and carefully vinegared rice of almost unbelievable delicacy), along with appetizer, soup, sashimi, and grilled items. What shows up will be food of such beautiful simplicity that you may have to pinch yourself to remember that you're in Las Vegas. The rice is so perfect, you can count the grains in your mouth as you're eating it, and the fish—everything from baby sea bass to kamashita (collar) fatty tuna—is a revelation, and an education, in seafood. This is purist sushi for people who enjoy parsing the differences in texture between cuts of yellowtail, or those who go gaga over ikura (salmon roe) and kawahagi (leather blow fish).

The Japanese credo seems to be: Get out of the way and let the ingredient speak for itself. Seasonings and heat are always applied with a minimalist's touch, and whatever accents there are should, literally, barely touch the food. Thus do these chefs dedicate their lives to crafting each bite into something exquisite, a piece of food that creates a bond between the animal, the chef, and the customer. It's a bond that all chefs hope to achieve, but that Japanese chefs have turned into an art form. "Yui" roughly translates into that "unity between the chef and his diners," according to Gen-san. Put yourself in his hands and you'll feel the connection for yourself.

GET THIS

Nigiri sushi; omakase menu; Wagyu beef.

SEA SCALLOPS AT PAMPLONA

TOP TEN RESTAURANTS

Las Vegas is really two towns in one: the tourist corridor of downtown and the Strip, and off the Strip, where locals live and play.

Locals are famous for disdaining the Strip, and visitors rarely leave their comfortable hotels to go exploring the suburbs. Admittedly, 10 years ago, there wasn't much to explore, but these days, some top chefs in the neighborhoods can go turbot to turbot with anything the casinos are serving. And since locals are always asking me about my favorite off-Strip places, I thought it was high time to give credit to our burgeoning neighborhood restaurant scene and break out our Top Ten into two distinctive lists.

Also for the first time, I'm ranking the Top Ten according to my personal ratings of where to get the best experiences in food, service, and atmosphere. Obviously, these are highly subjective. The differences between the actual food on the plate at Twist versus Le Cirque, for instance, are so minuscule as to be almost undiscernible to all but the most trained palate. And then, after eating at these places back to back to back, even I get confused.

Still, on any night of the week, on average, in the following 20 restaurants, you'll have the best overall experience, taking into account everything from the view to the dessert wines.

Put another way, if the world's greatest gourmet came to town and asked me to take him/her on a month-long tour of the best restaurants on the Strip, these are the ones I'd hit, in order.

ON THE STRIP

Joël Robuchon
Restaurant Guy Savoy
Le Cirque
Twist by Pierre Gagnaire
Sage
Bazaar Meat
'e' by José Andrés
Cipriani
Mott 32
Bardot Brasserie

OFF THE STRIP

Off-the-Strip restaurants are different animals entirely.

Gone are the casino money and thousands of customers funneling past your front door daily. Spending millions on décor and expecting a similar return on your dollar are out of the question. Instead, it's open on a shoestring and hang on for dear life. Out in the neighborhoods, it's sink or swim every day of the week and locally owned eateries struggle mightily against the currents of greedy landlords, clueless real estate developers, and character-less franchises.

No sane person would try to make a living feeding a public constantly racing to the bottom of the food trough (just look at all the cars parked in front of all-you-can-eat Asian buffets and Applebee's), but these operations are just crazy enough to buck those tides, as they try to upgrade what Las Vegans are eating. They deserve not only your business, but also a medal for making this town a much more civilized place in which to live. Here's my off-the-Strip list, in order.

Ferraro's Italian Restaurant and Wine Bar
Raku/Raku Sweets
Yui Edomae Sushi
EDO Tapas & Wine
Other Mama
EATT Gourmet Bistro
Sparrow + Wolf
Mordeo Boutique Wine Bar
Partage
Esther's Kitchen

LE CAVIAR AT JOEL ROBUCHON

John Curtas

CLOSE, BUT NO CIGAR

Keeping the framework of "52 Essential" cuts both ways: It makes our book more manageable for you, but it also eliminates a lot of worthy contenders for the top four-dozen-plus restaurants. All of the following are excellent in their own ways; it's only because of the competition or the passage of time that they can no longer be considered "essential."

Allegro (Wynn Las Vegas)
(702) 770-2040

Hearty Neapolitan cuisine in a sexy setting. Only the plethora of great new Italians knocked it out of the top 52.

Carbone (Aria at CityCenter)
(877) 230-2742

Insanely expensive over-the-top Italian with a lot of flair. Go hungry and with a group.

Chengdu Taste
3950 Schiff Drive
(702) 437-7888

Serious Szechuan tucked behind Spring Mountain Road.

CRISPY LION FISH (TILAPIA) AT CHENGDU TASTE

Hiroyoshi Japanese Cuisine
5900 W. Charleston Boulevard, #10
(702) 823-2110

Our fave neighborhood sushi. The bento box lunches on Fridays are to die for.

Picasso (Bellagio)
(702) 693-7223

So good for so long that it's like part of the furniture. The execution remains precise and those paintings are as spectacular as ever.

Blue Ribbon (Cosmopolitan)
(702) 698-7880

The best restaurant in Las Vegas for a crowd with diverse appetites. If you can't find something to like on this menu, you're either not human or a vegan.

Japaneiro
7315 W. Warm Springs Road, #170
(702) 260-8668

Japanese fusion (and great steaks) in an out-of-the-way location.

Jean Georges Steakhouse (Aria at CityCenter)
(702) 590-8660

Prime's little sibling is full of great steaks and a more diverse menu.

Julian Serrano (Aria at CityCenter)
(702) 590-8520

Totally terrific tapas; great cocktails, sherries, and wines too.

CUBAN TAPAS AT JULIAN SERRANO

Libertine Social (Mandalay Bay)
(702) 632-7558

Another crowd pleaser with maybe the best cocktails in town.

Morel's Steakhouse & Bistro (Palazzo)
(702) 607-6333

The best three-meal-a-day restaurant in Las Vegas. One of the best Caesar salads, too.

COBB SALAD AT MOREL'S STEAKHOUSE & BISTRO

MR CHOW (Caesars Palace)
(702) 731-7888

The restaurant critics love to hate, though I love it, just not enough to consider it "essential" any longer.

Prime (Bellagio)
(702) 693-7223

The menu never changes, but everything is excellent. It's also the most beautiful steakhouse in America, still, after 21 years.

Trattoria Nakamura-Ya
5040 W. Spring Mountain Road, #5
(702) 251-0022

I love the Japanese-Italian creations here, along with the feeling you're tucked into a Shinjuku alleyway when you're tucking into them. One of the many reasons our Chinatown is such a wonderful place to explore.

BOTTOM 10

Do you enjoy overpriced tourist traps? Tired food? Dated décor? Handing over hard-earned money to celebrity chefs phoning it in?

Then Las Vegas has you covered!

This city boasts dozens of the world's greatest restaurants, but it also hosts more than a few half-baked concepts, licensing deals with "name" chefs, and sad old war horses, and all exist solely to separate the uninformed and gullible from their cash.

As a public service, here are my selections for Vegas restaurants to avoid—and my reasons why.

10) Italian-American Club—An old saying goes, "The quality of an Italian restaurant is inversely proportional to the number of pictures of Frank Sinatra on the walls." There are *a lot* of pictures of Sinatra on these walls.

9) John Mull's Meats—Guy Fieri's taste in barbecue rivals his taste in haircuts. He came here once and Mull's has been trading off it ever since. This place is to 'cue what "Diners, Drive-ins and Dives" is to haute cuisine.

8) SW Steakhouse—SW stands for "Steve Wynn." He used to walk around his hotel with his testicles hanging out of his (too-short) tennis shorts. I'd rather stare at his ball sac than this wine list.

7) Piero's—The drinks at Piero's are huge and the conventioneers many. Pia Zadora performs here and her singing (and those drinks) will help you forget about the food. Neither can help with all those guys in Dockers and golf shirts.

John Curtas

6) Hell's Kitchen— A mecca for slack-jawed starfuckers who actually believe El Gordo has something to do with the joint besides slapping his name on the door. They have as much chance of seeing Ramsay here as you have of catching me at a monster truck rally.

5) Battista's Hole in the Wall—Italian food served in buckets to the hoi polloi who love garlic, soggy noodles, and unlimited soda pop masquerading as house wine. The pictures on the wall are a nice distraction from food, from which much distraction is needed.

4) Sara's—Billed as a "hidden supper club," what you get is a dark steakhouse and lots of attitude. Without the pretension, it would simply be forgettable. A serious miss that could've been a hit.

3) Michael's—In terms of price-to-value ratio, Michael's is the worst restaurant in town by a green-felt mile. The prices are stratospheric, service is metronomic, and the food soporific. For these insults, you will pay hundreds of dollars per person.

2) Giada's—Another licensing deal designed to rope in the rubes. Giada's face is everywhere—except for the kitchen and then only when cameras are around. If she's a chef, I'm an astronaut.

1) Momofuku—You've got to hand it to David Chang. He now runs a world-wide restaurant empire based on recipes that mirror his personality: overblown, bombastic, and boring.

CHICKEN SKEWER AT HATSUMI

Section II

Additional Recommendations

KABOB FEAST AT KHOURY'S

Additional Recommendations
Introduction

The second half of the book provides plentiful additional suggestions for Las Vegas' top restaurants in the many categories that readers, neighbors, colleagues, family, friends, and total strangers frequently ask us to recommend. Additionally, you'll find expanded sections on Chinatown, steakhouses, French restaurants, buffets, and burgers. Maps and a detailed index eliminate any challenge you might have for locating every eatery referenced in the book.

Note that Huntington Press (the publisher of the *Eating Las Vegas* series) also maintains LasVegasAdvisor.com, which covers the Las Vegas dining scene extensively. There you can find lengthy and constantly updated listings of cheap eats, local favorites, late-night dining spots, and additional meal options in more categories than appear here. And although I don't frequent the buffets, I have a huge amount of respect for the chefs who work in them and the customers who enjoy the ability to sample a lot of different food for one set price, and there had to be a buffet listing in this volume. Here again, input from the *Las Vegas Advisor* was paramount in identifying the city's best.

One quick word about locations. Each of the entries in this section includes an address and phone number. When a recommendation has two or three locations, it's noted, and when it has more than three, it's listed as "multiple locations." The address and phone for each are presented according to the following protocol. If there's an original or clearly dominant location, that's the one that's listed. And if not, the location that's geographically closest to the Strip is used. When a restaurant appears in more than one section, the location and phone are provided in the first listing only and subsequent listings refer back to the original.

BEEF TEPPAN YAKI AT TATSUJIN X

FOOD

CHINATOWN

When Chinatown Plaza opened in 1995—housing five restaurants and a smattering of shops—Spring Mountain Road was known mainly for its potholes. No one thought of this area as Chinatown and it was audacious of the developers to call it such. Twenty-five years later, I estimate I've eaten in more than 125 restaurants along Spring Mountain Road. All you can do is applaud their prescience and marvel at what this three-mile stretch of road has become.

At last count, more than 150 Asian restaurants line this avenue (and, it seems, triple that number of massage parlors and nail salons). These days, the whole stretch of street from Valley View to Jones is a veritable buffet of Asian eats and it's a must-stop on any foodie tour of Las Vegas. Intrepid gastronauts know this is where you come to get the real deal in Chinese barbecue, Japanese noodles, and giant bowls of whatever soup suits your fancy—all at astoundingly cheap prices.

Some notes on the following lists. For the most part, these are places I highly recommend and have visited multiple times, but remember that it's Chinatown, Jake, meaning: Owners change, chefs come and go, and you never really know what's going on. Also, Homie don't do no all-you-can-eat-anything, so those low-rent sushi joints are nowhere to be found in this book. I'm not big on conveyor-belt service either, preferring my food to be cooked to order, not spewed out wholesale from a kitchen in hopes someone will grab it. And while I'm at it, don't ask me for hot-pot recommendations. I'm more interested in minor-league Lithuanian soccer than I am in bubbling bowls of broth where everything tastes the same.

Finally, none of these joints are for picky eaters. The whole point of eating along Spring Mountain Road is that it's the closest you'll ever get to the real thing without a 14-hour flight across the Pacific. In some of these places, English is definitely a second language. In others, service is often perfunctory and not of the most professional quality. But arrive with an open mind and an adventuresome palate and you'll be an Asian maven in no time. But arrive with an open mind and adventuresome palate and you'll be an Asian maven in no time.

BEEF CHOW MEIN AT 88 NOODLE PAPA

88 Noodle Papa
4276 Spring Mountain Road
(702) 550-0717; (725) 251-2078

In the spanking new Shanghai Plaza, another authentic Chinese noodle parlor with a very pleasant staff and easy-to-navigate menu. The Food Gal loves their Hainan chicken, I come for the beef chow mein and won ton soups.

Asian BBQ & Noodle
3400 S. Jones Boulevard, #5C
(702) 202-3636

Go well before noon or mid-afternoon if you want to get a seat. Max Jacobson, one of the original authors of this book, endorsed this as the best Chinese barbecue in Vegas and I have no reason to argue with him. Closed Fridays. (Yes, Fridays. Oh, those crazy Asians.)

BBQ King
5650 Spring Mountain Road
(702) 364-8688

Cash only. Cantonese only.

John Curtas

Big Wong
5040 Spring Mountain Road, #6
(702) 368-6808

Beef noodle soups to beat the band.

Capital Seafood Restaurant
4215 Spring Mountain Road
(702) 227-3588

In the original Chinatown Plaza, going strong for 20 years. Superb Cantonese lobster stir-fries at half the cost you'd pay a mile to the east.

Chengdu Taste (see "Close, But No Cigar" page 129)

China Mama (Essential 52: see page 32)

Chubby Cattle
3400 S. Jones Boulevard
(702) 868-8808

Conveyor-belt hot pot is the mode at this new Mongolian eatery. Some of it is hokey, but the extensive menu has legitimate—and sometimes esoteric—Asian surprises in store.

WAGYU YUKKE AT CHUBBY CATTLE

Additional Recommendations

J&J Szechuan Cuisine
5700 Spring Mountain Road
(702) 876-5983

My favorite, old-school, go-to Szechuan now has serious competition, but still shines.

Joyful House
4601 Spring Mountain Road
(702) 889-8881

One of those truly terrible places that's been around forever. Strictly for the sweet-and-sour-pork crowd.

Miàn Sichuan Noodle
4355 Spring Mountain Road
(702) 483-6531

Straight from the San Gabriel Valley comes this offshoot featuring the fiery mouth-numbing noodle soup/stews of Sichuan. Guaranteed you'll be the only *gwailo* in the joint.

New Asian BBQ Tan Tung Ky
5150 Spring Mountain Road
(702) 202-2262

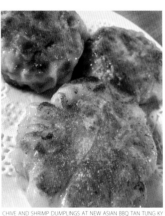

Opened in 2019, this place immediately announced itself as the best Chinese barbecue on Spring Mountain Road, along with very good, if somewhat standard, dim sum. You'll be the only round-eye in the joint, but don't let that deter you. Service is friendly and super-fast.

CHIVE AND SHRIMP DUMPLINGS AT NEW ASIAN BBQ TAN TUNG KY

NURO Bistro
4255 S. Durango Drive, #110
(702) 901-4609

You have to travel all the way out to Durango Drive to get it, but this is the best Hainanese chicken in town.

Orchids Garden

5845 W. Sahara Avenue
(702) 631-3839

For years the sign out front read, "Chinese food to go in rear." For a decade, the dim sum was lame and the place was on life support. Now it's one of our best and crowded all the time. Go figure.

CLAMS IN BLACK BEAN SAUCE AT ORCHIDS GARDEN

Ping Pang Pong (Gold Coast)
(702) 247-8136

It's not really in Chinatown. But it's nearby and serves some of the best dim sum in town. Unfortunately, you have to brave the environs of the Gold Coast to get to it, and go early: By noon every day, the place is full of Asians and Caucasians fighting for a table.

Shang Artisan Noodle
4983 W. Flamingo Road
(702) 888-3292

Dinner and a show! Or lunch and a cooking lesson. No matter when you arrive, they'll be hand-pulling noodles in that wonderful piece of sleight-of-hand that makes for delicious Chinese lamian. Don't miss the spicy wontons or the beef pancake.

The Noodle Man
6870 S. Rainbow Boulevard, #101
(702) 823-3333

Not strictly in Chinatown, but wonderful hand-pulled ribbons are thrown and cut out in the open (they make a show out of it). Noodle Man is a southwest Vegas favorite for its delicious soups and other noodle-based dishes.

Veggie House
5115 Spring Mountain Road, #203
(702) 431-5802

A full menu of classic Chinese dishes and some not-so-classic house specials (try the crispy spicy eggplant), all using vegetarian ingredients only. Open for lunch and dinner, dine in or take out.

Yummy Rice
4266 Spring Mountain Road
(702) 331-3789

The conceit here is bowls of rice in a hot clay pot topped with eel, egg, pork, or a combo of ingredients. The vibe is very "Hong Kong café" and the bill so small, you won't believe it.

Yun Nan Garden
3934 Schiff Drive
(702) 869-8885

Hidden on Schiff Dr. behind a Chinatown strip mall, Yun Nan holds its own with neighbor Chengdu Taste. Get the good noodle soups or take out from a unique fast-serve counter offering seaweed, neck bones, pigs ears, and a dozen more exotic selections.

Japanese

Hachi Japanese Yakitori Izakaya
3410 S. Jones Boulevard
(702) 227-9300

Another newcomer to our izakaya revolution, Hachi is well-run and more inventive than most.

Hiroyoshi Japanese Cuisine (see "Close, But No Cigar" page 129)

Our favorite neighborhood sushi. Small, creative, pristine, and personal: very much like you find in Japan.

John Curtas

Ichiza
4355 Spring Mountain Road, #205
(702) 367-3151

A grimy second-floor joint that's seen better days, but the food is pretty nifty.

Izakaya Go
3775 Spring Mountain Road
(702) 247-1183

Sake houses have been popping up like cherry blossoms in April lately, and this is one of the best. The menu is huge, the fish impeccable, and the robatayaki remarkable.

SASHIMI AT IZAKAYA GO

Japanese Curry Zen
5020 Spring Mountain Road, #1
(702) 985-1192

If price to value were the only criterion, Zen would beat out Guy Savoy and Joël Robuchon for the best in town. Good gyoza, great spinach curry, insanely cheap prices.

Kabuto (Essential 52: see page 60)

Kaiseki Yuzu (Essential 52: see page 62)

Additional Recommendations

Monta Ramen
5030 Spring Mountain Road
(702) 367-4600

Still the gold standard for authentic ramen in Vegas, this extremely popular nook started Chinatown on its upswing. The dashi (broth) is supple and sublime. Get there early, as it packs in a crowd regularly, though it's no longer the only noodle shogun in town.

AGEDASHI TOFU AT RAKU

Raku/Sweets Raku (Essential 52: see page 98)

Ramen Hashi
5808 Spring Mountain Road, #109
(702) 202-1238

Fifteen seats and superb chicken shio and shoyu ramen await you. For the record, this lighter-style ramen is the Food Gal's favorite in town.

Ramen KoBo
7040 S. Durango Drive, #104
(702) 489-7788

The owners of perennial-favorite Monta are making their own noodles in this suburban location. The excellent dashi-filled bowls are much spicier here than at the mother restaurant.

John Curtas

Ramen KoBo Plus
3889 Spring Mountain Road
(702) 202-1177

Ramen is everywhere in Chinatown; it's time it got a little competition from these thick, chewy, rectangular, and soft wheat-starch noodles from Marugame, Japan. At peak hours, you'll have to wait in line. It's worth it.

Ramen Sora
4490 Spring Mountain Road
(702) 685-1011

Sapporo ramen—rich, nutty, and sweet—is perfect for a cold day in the desert. Monta's broth may be more refined, but Ramen Sora fills the bill any season (but summer).

Ramen Tatsu
3400 S. Jones Boulevard
(702) 629-7777

Another ramen joint that will do in a pinch when the two superstars, Monta and Ramen Sora, are full.

Soho Japanese Restaurant
7377 S. Jones Boulevard
(702) 776-7778

John Lee's crowd-pleasing Japanese has something for everyone, but his omakase is the hidden superstar.

Sojo Ramen
7737 S. Jones Boulevard
(702) 987-9624

Right next door to its full-service parent, this offspring sports some serious noodles.

Sushi Kame Omakase & Kaiseki
3616 W. Spring Mountain Road
(702) 771-0122

Serious kaiseki meals starting at a serious price ($200/pp).

Additional Recommendations

Tatsujin X (Essential 52: see page 110)

Trattoria Nakamura-Ya (see "Close, But No Cigar" page 132)

Wafuu pasta, a Japanese take on Italian food, is the specialty here and dish after dish is fascinating and fun. Order off the big chalkboard and expect some of the most interesting food in town.

UNI TOMATO CREAM AT TRATTORIA NAKAMURA-YA

Yui Edomae Sushi (Essential 52: see page 124)

Korean

8oz Korean Steakhouse & Bar
4545 Spring Mountain Road, #B105
(702) 909-3121

The newest entrant in our upgraded Korean meat sweepstakes is also the best. The name comes from the larger portion sizes here versus what gets served in Seoul. Me thinks even Kim Jong Un would approve. Cool bar, too.

John Curtas

Hobak Korean BBQ
5808 Spring Mountain Road, #101
(702) 257-1526

Korean 'cue took a big leap forward in the past year and this cacophonous casual spot led the way with better beef and upgraded banchan. If only they'd turn the music down.

Honey Pig (2 locations)
4725 Spring Mountain Road, #K / 9550 S. Eastern Avenue, #100
(702) 876-8308 / (702) 979-9719

Panchan cooking at its finest. Which means you do all the work on an inverted wok, holding everything from all of those obscure cuts of Korean beef to the last squid standing. Come with a crowd and you'll enjoy yourself. Come as a deuce and you'll wonder what hit you.

Kkulmat Korean Kitchen
5600 Spring Mountain Road, #A
(702) 333-4845

Koreans love to show you pictures of their food on the menu and throughout the restaurant. We gringos appreciate the photos and the food. Pilgrims from both sides of the Pacific will love this simple homey fare without all the choreography you find in Korean steakhouses.

Lee's Korean BBQ
6820 Spring Mountain Road
(702) 388-0488

Mr. Lee (owner of a local chain of liquor stores more known for quantity than quality) owns this joint as well and highly recommends it! Or at least that's what the billboards all around town say. Personally, as soon as I see an "all-you-can-eat" sign, I turn the car around.

MaGal BBQ
4240 Spring Mountain Road
(702) 476-8833

Of all our new, higher-toned, franchise, Korean BBQ joints, this one has the most Seoul. (Sorry.)

Tofu Hut
3920 Spring Mountain Road
(702) 257-0072

Good cheap bowls of Korean soups that all taste alike to me.

YuXiang Korean-Chinese Cuisine
7729 S. Rainbow Blvd. #3
(702) 790-3474

Korean-Chinese food is a thing, and it's a thing that's finally come to Las Vegas. The noodles are thick, the sauces are practically black, and the crispy beef is out of this world. Don't miss the jjajangmyeon.

John Curtas

Thai

Chuchote Thai Bistro & Dessert
4105 W. Sahara Avenue
(702) 685-7433

The newest entry in our "Thai one on" universe is a classy little joint with upscale dishes and a take-no-prisoners southern Thai vibe. The desserts are frozen and inventive and you'll need them to quell the heat.

D E Thai Kitchen
1108 S. 3rd Street
(702) 979-9121

Terrific street Thai in a teeny tiny space. Of all the great Thai restaurants in Vegas, this is where I eat most often.

Krung Siam Thai
3755 Spring Mountain Rd., #102
(702) 735-9485

YELLOW CURRY CRAB AT D E THAI KITCHEN

Old-fashioned Thai.

Kung Fu Thai & Chinese Restaurant
3505 S. Valley View Boulevard
(702) 247-4120

The granddaddy of Thai restaurants in town. It still does that over-sweet-thing that American Thai restaurants can't get away from, but it's a solid choice, and the yen ta foe (pink noodle soup) is pretty darn scrumptious.

Lamaii (Essential 52: see page 68)

Le Thai/Le Thai 2
523 Fremont Street / 2202 W. Charleston Boulevard
(702) 778-0888 / (702) 675-3892

Chef Dan Coughlin's homage to Thailand's street eats can be enjoyed on Fremont Street, where you can sit down, or on W. Charleston, where you can take out. It's more fun for us aging Boomers to take his three-color curry home, where the only drunk I have to dodge is myself.

Ocha Thai Cuisine
1201 S. Las Vegas Boulevard, #150
(702) 386-8631

Traditional Thai a cut or three above all that gloppy sweet stuff you find in the 'burbs. Since 1989, Ocha has been holding down the fort downtown for lovers of the real deal in moo dad deaw (pork jerky) and tod mun (fish cake).

Weera Thai Kitchen (Essential 52: see page 120)
4276 Spring Moutain Road, #105 / 3839 W. Sahara Avenue, #9
(702) 485-1688 / (702) 873-8749

It's not technically in Chinatown, but the Sahara Avenue location rates a major wave for its northern Thai specialties, regional variety—Laos and Issan are represented—and beautifully crafted duck dishes.

GIANT RIVER PRAWNS AT WEERA THAI KITCHEN

John Curtas

Vietnamese

No matter how much I try to discern the differences in this or that pho (or the menus, for that matter), I never can. So, rather than strain my brain attempting to differentiate among these places, all I can do is vouch for them. All of these are good, if remarkably similar. District One and The Black Sheep are great.

District One (Essential 52: see page 38)

Pho 87
3620 S. Jones Boulevard
(702) 233-8787

Pho Aimie
8390 S. Rainbow Boulevard
(702) 776-7017

Pho Kim Long
4023 Spring Mountain Road
(702) 220-3613

Pho Saigon #8
9055 S. Eastern Avenue, #1C
(702) 629-3100

Pho Sing Sing
2550 S. Rainbow Boulevard
(702) 380-2999

Pho Vietnam
4215 Spring Mountain Road, #B201
(702) 227-8618

The Black Sheep (Essential 52: see page 112)
8680 W. Warm Springs Road
(702) 954-3998

Viet Noodle Bar
5288 Spring Mountain Road, #106
(702) 750-9898

Additional Recommendations

THE "LUCAS" AT BAJAMAR SEAFOOD & TACOS

DOWNTOWN DINING

Downtown is a gastronomic destination in its own right these days. Six years ago, I would've said you're crazy if you uttered those words. But things have been booming and options will continue to expand as everything from wine bars to wood-fired pizzas are on the horizon. Main and East Fremont streets are the epicenters of this epicurean revolution, and though bleak some surroundings may be, once you duck inside any of these eateries, you'll find delightful meals and hand-tooled food aplenty.

7th & Carson
616 E. Carson Avenue, #110
(702) 868-3355

Elevated pub grub at a location we can never quite remember (get it?).

Bajamar Seafood & Tacos
1615 S. Las Vegas Boulevard
(702) 331-4266

Good Mexican food used to be harder to find downtown than a slot junkie with a good credit score. These straight-from-Baja tacos immediately changed that. Ignore the surroundings and dive in.

Carson Kitchen (Essential 52: see page 30)
124 S. 6th Street, #100
(702) 473-9523

CK started the downtown dining revolution five years ago and it's still going strong. Those veal meatballs, the oxtail risotto, and the glazed-donut bread pudding never get old.

Casa Don Juan (mulitple locations)
1204 S. Main Street
(702) 384-8070

An old reliable with a large menu and a huge following. The tortillas, carnitas, and great service keep us coming back.

Additional Recommendations

D E Thai Kitchen (see page 151)

Forget the regular menu and order off the (not-so) secret menu on the chalkboard. If there're better kua gling (spicy ground pork) or Thai soft-shell crabs in town, we haven't found them.

EAT
707 E. Carson Avenue
(702) 534-1515

Wonderful breakfast and lunch—to die for flapjacks and heavenly hash.

Esther's Kitchen (Essential 52: see page 48)

1130 S. Casino Center Boulevard, #110
(702) 570-7864

I eat here so often, they ought to name a booth after me.

Evel Pie
508 Fremont Street
(702) 840-6460

Downtown is blessed with four good pizza joints, and it all started with Evel Pie.

Good Pie
725 S. Las Vegas Boulevard, #140
(702) 844-2700

HAMCHI CRUDO AT ESTHER'S KITCHEN

Nothing more than a counter, some deck ovens, and an assortment of the best slices in Vegas. By the time you read this, they will have opened a full-service pizza restaurant on Charleston near Main, much to the rejoicing of pizza mavens everywhere.

John Curtas

Hatsumi (Essential 52: see page 54)
1028 Fremont Street, #100
(702) 268-8939

Robatayaki on East Fremont? Yep, and it's great. Fine sake list, too.

Jammyland Cocktail Bar & Reggae Kitchen
1121 S. Main Street
(702) 800-9298

The drinks here are so good, they make me wish I were an alcoholic. A booze-absorbing menu of (mostly) Jamaican food is just the thing after a few of them.

Ocha Thai Cuisine (see page 152)

A family-run oasis of good Thai cooking for decades.

Old Soul (Essential 52: see page 88)

The odds are against Old Soul, but Natalie Young's food is so good, we don't care. Take the time to find it and you'll fall in love.

LIVER AND ONIONS AT OLD SOUL

Oscar's Steakhouse
1 S. Main Street
(702) 386-7227

Oscar Goodman is an iconic figure in Las Vegas. His steakhouse doesn't quite match his outsized reputation, but new chef Ben Jenkins is on a mission to change all that.

Pop Up Pizza (Plaza Hotel)
(702) 366-0049

The only thing wrong with Pop Up Pizza is its customers. Most of them take a gander at these superior pies and wonder where the Dominos is.

PublicUs
1126 Fremont Street
(702) 331-5500

I constantly debate the relative merits of PublicUs versus Vesta like a man who can't decide between his wife and his mistress. I resolve this argument by alternating between them, just like I did in 1999.

Santos Guisados Tacos & Beer
616 E. Carson Street, #140
(702) 826-3515

These guisado (braised meat) tacos are in a class by themselves. Good beers and a full bar in a place about the size of a studio apartment.

The Goodwich
900 S. Las Vegas Boulevard
(702) 910-8681

We have dreams about the Reuben-ish and the Patty. How good do sandwiches have to be for you to dream about them?

REUBEN-ISH AT THE GOODWICH

John Curtas

The Kitchen at Atomic (Essential 52: see page 114)
927 Fremont Street
(702) 534-3223

Jackson Stamper's food might be too hip for the room, but it suits us just fine. One of the best steaks (and rum-brined pork chops) in town, too.

FISH N CHIPS AT THE SMASHED PIG

The Smashed Pig
509 Fremont Street
(702) 444-7816

Ignore the Fremont Street fanny-packers and duck in for a black-and-tan and the fish and chips.

VegeNation
618 Carson Avenue, #120 / 10075 S. Eastern Avenue
(702) 366-8515 / (702) 527-7663

If you insist, there's a vegan restaurant downtown—the best vegan restaurant in town, actually. I've actually eaten here, more than once (hangs head in shame).

Vesta Coffee Roasters
1114 S. Casino Center Boulevard, #1
(702) 685-1777

See comment on PublicUs. And please don't mention anything to the Food Gal (my current wife).

Additional Recommendations

CHATEAUBRIAND AT SCOTCH 80 PRIME

HIGH STEAKS:
THE BEST BEEF IN VEGAS

How do you judge a steakhouse?

Is it the quality of the beef? How well they age it? Cook it? The variety of the side dishes? Or is it all about the wine list to you? Or the décor—dark, masculine, and clubby, or light, bright, and more modern? Maybe you demand tenderness at all costs? (For the record: a big mistake, since a superior, intensely mineral-rich, roasted-to-exquisite-beefiness strip sirloin should have a fair amount of chew to it.)

Maybe you're service-obsessive. Many people are. For them, the warmth of the welcome and speediness of the staff keep them coming back.

Perhaps you're a sucker for big bones. Or the type that occasionally gets a hankering for a (less expensive) hanger steak. Or someone who prefers cuts served in less traditional ways. Or likes a lot of folderol with their cholesterol.

Whoever you are, it's a fair bet that you're a conspicuous carnivore and nothing gets your juices flowing like tucking into a haunch of well-marbled steer muscle. If that sounds up your alley, you might consider moving to Las Vegas. Because next to the Big Apple, no city on Earth has better steakhouses than Sin City. And on any given night, I'll put our chef-driven joints up against anything New York City can throw at us.

True, for sheer volume, historical precedent, and breadth of menu options, nothing beats what you find in NYC, but if you look at many Big Apple classics, you'll find a number that haven't changed a thing on their menu in decades. If you close your eyes when you walk into Peter Luger, Keen's, Spark's, Wolfgang's, Gallagher's, Palm Too, and others, then gaze only at your plate, you won't be able to tell whether you're in 1978, 1998, or 2018. Yes, the steaks are magnificent and there's no replacing the testosterone-charged atmosphere in any of them, but in many ways, you're eating in a museum.

Not so in present-day Las Vegas, where the massive meat emporia give the chefs a lot of latitude to play with their food. These days, seasonal sides are all the rage and chefs like Matthew Hurley (CUT), Robert Moore (Prime), Sean Griffin (Jean-Georges), Ronnie Rainwater (Delmonico), and Daniel Ontiveros (Scotch 80 Prime) make things interesting from season to season, with a plethora of veggies,

Additional Recommendations

seafood, and other succulents that can keep even the fussiest gastronome unbored and happy.

Every top house in Vegas now features mind-blowing dry-aged steaks and multiple A-4 and A-5 cuts from Japan), we leave previously preeminent beef bastions like Chicago, Dallas, and Miami running in third, fourth, and fifth places. And if you do that eye-closing plate-gazing thing again, you can't tell the difference between the best of our beef and anything you bite into in midtown Manhattan.

STEAK TARTARE AT BAVETTE'S STEAKHOUSE & BAR

Bavette's Steakhouse & Bar (Park MGM)

The newest entry into our high-steaks competition, this Chicago off-shoot is clubby, masculine, dark (and I mean *dark*), and old school in all the best ways. The strip steak is a showstopper, as are the burger and salads. You may need a flashlight to see your food and you'll definitely need a defibrillator when you get the bill.

Bazaar Meat (Essential 52: see page 24)

CUT (Essential 52: see page 36)

Delmonico Steakhouse (Venetian)
(702) 414-3737

Like a few other time-worn and treasured Las Vegas restaurants, Delmonico has been around so long we tend to take it for granted. But like Emeril's, this venerable spot is due for a salute. It opened on May 3, 1999, and for nearly 18 years has been rendering drop-dead delicious versions of the food that made Emeril Lagasse famous.

Some people call it a steakhouse, but that doesn't tell half the story. I'd argue that, on any given night, the seafood here is every bit the equal of what's served by its big sister in the MGM Grand. I'd also argue that the gumbo is a dead ringer for the Bam Man's fare in N'Awlins itself and that the lobster bisque and crispy fried oysters are as good as you'll find 1,000 miles from the Gulf of Mexico. Of course, the steaks are first-rate too—especially the Nebraska-bred Piedmontese strip and the dry-aged cuts—but Executive Chef Ronnie Rainwaters' apple-cured, applewood-smoked, bone-in bacon and one of the best Caesar salads in the business has me licking my chops every time I walk in the place.

RIB EYE AT BAZAAR MEAT

Additional Recommendations

163

Gordon Ramsay Steak (Paris Las Vegas)
(702) 946-4663

Every restaurant in Vegas would be a steakhouse if it could be, and Ramsay, one of the best classical chefs in the business, was smart to recognize that fact. This, and his excellent burger joint at Planet Hollywood, keep him waist deep in pounds sterling, but be forewarned, not all Gordon Ramsay restaurants in Vegas are created equal. Mr. Profanity lent his name, but none of his talent, to the Gordon Ramsay Pub & Grill in Caesars. Stick with his steakhouse and burger palace if you want to retain a modicum of respect for what he once was.

Prime (see "Close, But No Cigar" page 131)

With a décor more akin to a (huge) French dining salon than an American steakhouse, this Bellagio mainstay does the Jean-George Vongerichten brand proud. The intensive-care service never misses a beat and the expanded lounge and outdoor patio area provide a casual retreat for those not wanting to invest in a first-class steak dinner. As good as the steaks are, the seafood and Parmesan-crusted chicken separate this gem from its competitors.

Scotch 80 Prime (Palms)
(702) 942-7777

What once was N9NE at the Palms has been re-done and re-vitalized into a first-class meat emporium where the design finally equals the food. It's big and open, but also warm and sexy, with a whisky bar par excellence, caviar service, and enough tweaked steakhouse classics—Caesar, wedge, crab cake, lobster bisque—to keep even the most jaded carnivore happy. Very few steakhouses let a chef put his personality into the goods, but Daniel Ontiveros' spin on these staples, such as his dry-aged steaks and chocolate bacon, is worth a special trip. Best of all, the prices are slightly underneath those a mile to the east.

Strip House (Planet Hollywood)
(702) 737-5200

Strip House (tucked into a corner of Planet Hollywood) is harder to find than a hooker who works on credit, but I love it just the same. If it were more accessible, I'd be in once a week for the goose-fat

John Curtas

potatoes alone. It also might make the best béarnaise sauce in town. Since I can resist anything but temptation, I'm glad it's such a pain in the ass to get to.

StripSteak (Mandalay Bay)
(702) 632-7200

Every time I go to Strip Steak, I have a helluva meal and a whale of a good time. Then I forget about it for another year or so, because I remember I hate the décor (it looks like a coffee shop), which causes me to neglect it until my memories fade and I overlook the ugliness and return for another great steak. Does this make any sense to you? Me neither. Good side dishes, too.

Honorable Mention

Circus Circus Steakhouse (if you can stand the hotel), Lawry's The Prime Rib (an old standby that still delivers), Charlie Palmer Steak (a recent upgrade has got this place humming again), Hank's Fine Steaks (if you can stand driving to Henderson), Oscar's Steakhouse (the food has improved and you can't beat the décor, or the booze), and Vic & Anthony's (some people swear by V&A's; I can swear only that it's the one decent place to eat at the Golden Nugget).

Bargain Steaks

Las Vegas is famous for its bargain steak and prime rib dinners, many of which run off and on as promotions in the casinos. The following are ongoing best bets for finding a good steak for under $20: Ellis Island, Herbs & Rye, Hitchin' Post Saloon and Steakhouse, Irene's, Jackson's Bar & Grill, and Rincon de Buenos Aires.

OFF-THE-MENU STEAK SPECIAL AT ELLIS ISLAND

Additional Recommendations

FRENCH

Las Vegas is blessed with more great French food than anywhere in America that isn't New York City. The food our French chefs turn out every day, be it in a restaurant, brasserie, or bistro, tastes like you're a stone's throw from the Champs-Élysées. We had our own little French Revolution here (2005-2010), which saw names like Robuchon, Boulud, Gagnaire, and Savoy plant their flags on these desert shores and their standards of excellence continue to be the bar by which all chefs measure themselves.

Bardot Brasserie (Essential 52: see page 22)

Bouchon (Essential 52: see page 28)

Café Breizh
3555 S. Fort Apache Road, #141
(702) 209-3472

Small, but exquisite. A limited selection of croissants, tarts, crêpes, and brioche doesn't keep these from being the best you'll find this far from the Left Bank.

Delices Gourmands French Bakery
3620 W. Sahara Avenue
(702) 331-2526

A couple of miles west of the Strip in a strip mall that's seen better days, you'll find one of our better bakeries. Not much on décor, but the breads are *très fantastique* and the crêpes, huge baguette sandwiches, and canelés de Bordeaux are the genuine articles.

EATT Gourmet Bistro (Essential 52: see page 42)

Eiffel Tower Restaurant (Paris Las Vegas)
(702) 948-6937

They probably do more weddings here than in all other Vegas restaurants combined. Solid (if unimaginative) French fare amidst one of the most dramatic settings at which you will ever swoon over a soufflé.

Additional Recommendations

Joël Robuchon (Essential 52: see page 58)

L'Atelier de Joël Robuchon (Essential 52: see page 66)

Le Cirque (Essential 52: see page 70)

Marché Bacchus (Essential 52: see page 76)

Mg Patisserie and Café
6385 S. Rainbow Boulevard, #101
(702) 220-4860

Michael Gillet's minuscule patisserie (right down the street from Rosallie) gives South Rainbow residents a veritable cornucopia of custards, croissants, and cakes to fatten up on.

Mon Ami Gabi (Paris Las Vegas)
(702) 944-4224

Best people-watching in town (on the patio); best three-meals-a day French restaurant in town.

Oh La La French Bistro
(Essential 52: see page 86)

Patisserie Manon
8751 W. Charleston Boulevard, #110
(702) 586-2666

Popular west-side neighborhood spot on the cusp of Summerlin. It doesn't hold a candle to Rosallie or Bouchon, but its macaroons and quiches will do in a pinch.

SOLE MEUNIÈRE AT OH LA LA FRENCH BISTRO

Picasso (see "Close, But No Cigar" page 129)

Restaurant Guy Savoy (Essential 52: see page 100)

John Curtas

NORD SANDWICH AT ROSALLIE LE FRENCH CAFE

Rosallie Le French Café
6090 S. Rainbow Boulevard
(702) 998-4121

This tiny bakery sits like an island of ethereal pastries, quiches, sandwiches, and desserts in a sea of empty lots and ugly office buildings in the southwest part of town. Once you step through the doors, you're transported to the type of homey little café you find all over France. The quiches are probably the best in town and the croissants, pain au chocolat, and sandwiches take a back seat to no one's. My rule of thumb at Rosallie is, "If it looks good, it is good," and everything in their pastry case always looks great. Really good coffee too, and wine!

Suzuya Pastries & Crepes
7225 S. Durango Drive, #101
(702) 432-1990

Remarkable pastries in the southwestern part of town.

The Real Crepe
7595 W. Washington Avenue, #160
(702) 701-4516

A little slice of Brittany on the cusp of Summerlin. The buckwheat galettes and dessert crêpes are the real deal and a steal.

Twist (Essential 52: see page 116)

Additional Recommendations

BUFFETS

Las Vegas has been the Buffet Capital of the World for more than 70 years (since 1946 when the Buckaroo Buffet, Vegas' first midnight "chuckwagon," appeared at the El Rancho Vegas). Why do visitors and locals flock to them like lemmings to a cliff? Well, this city is synonymous with excess—24-hour gambling, drinking, carousing, and eating. Yet while not every visitor is inclined to dive headlong into blackjack, booze, and all-night blowouts, gluttony has never seemed tangled in moral issues.

If you're looking for quantity over quality and you're okay with starchy sauces over mystery meat and fish, gloppy casseroles, and salads that come from 55-gallon drums, just head for the cheapest buffet you can find. Still, some of the less expensive spreads are, actually, recommendable.

Some of the best come from the Boyd casino group, including those at the Orleans, Gold Coast, Suncoast, and the downtown favorite, Main Street Station, along with Station Casinos' Feast Buffets, which are even better on a price-to-quality comparison. In 2018, Station brought on revamped buffets at the Palms and Palace Station that the *Las Vegas Advisor* ranks as the top two buffet choices in town for value. Both are included in the best-buffet list that follows, along with the city's best when price isn't a consideration.

Bacchanal Buffet (Caesars Palace)
(702) 731-7928

Ultra-modern 600-seat room with a reported 500 selections in nine different cuisines. It's so popular, even at the price, that they sell line passes for a mere $25 per person to people who want to avoid the long waits (one of only two line-pass-for-a-price buffets I know of; the other is the Cosmopolitan). The seafood station is the most varied and high-quality in town.

The Buffet (Bellagio)
(702) 693-8111

The Buffet at Bellagio made a big splash when it opened in 1996 and hasn't missed a beat since. You can count on the food being high-quality and it's the only buffet in town with a chef's table with a specialty menu that uses the freshest seasonal products. And there's a little bar play: Walk past the epic lines waiting to get in and see if there are any seats at the bar. If so, claim them! You pay the bartender at the end of the meal and your drinks are always right there.

The Buffet (Wynn Las Vegas)
(702) 770-3340

This buffet competes for best in Vegas. Fifteen action stations, including a whole rotisserie wall, a first-of-its-kind-in-North-America parrilla (grill), a chocolate fountain in which bakers dip an assortment of sweets, Frank Sinatra's family recipe for spaghetti and meatballs, plus short ribs, roast lamb, duck-leg cassoulet, and dim sum. It also caters to vegetarian/vegan, gluten-free, and diabetic diets.

Studio B (M Resort)
(702) 797-1000

M puts out a huge selection of more than 200 items and everything is restocked immediately. With the hordes of hungry this buffet attracts, how they keep up with it is a constant wonderment. Best of all, the prices are low for such a high-end spread. Only the Friday night seafood dinner is up there in price with the best gourmet superbuffets on the Strip. And *those* don't include unlimited beer and wine in the price, like this one does.

Wicked Spoon (Cosmopolitan)
(702) 698-7870

With more than 13,000 reviews on Yelp and TripAdvisor averaging four stars, this buffet is obviously a standout. It also receives a number of editor's picks as best buffet in Las Vegas. Many selections come in individual portions in little bowls and pots, so you don't have to scoop anything yourself, overload your plate, or overeat any one item. That said, the prime rib cuts and cracked king crab legs are big and abundant. One unusual carving-station item is the roasted bone marrow (reportedly super good for you). Definitely save room for dessert; the choices are too many to list and too good for spoiler alerts. And try the express take-out: $25 to load a container with as much as you can.

John Curtas

A.Y.C.E. Buffet (Palms)
(702) 942-7777

As part of a huge renovation of the Palms, Station Casinos unveiled the A.Y.C.E. Buffet in early 2018 with a potent small-plates selection reminiscent of the Cosmopolitan's Wicked Spoon, though for less than half the price. Along with American staples, there's a big selection of multi-national offerings that include Moroccan lamb, Singapore noodles, General Tso chicken, Mongolian beef, kalbi, coq au vin, and even shakshouka, an African egg dish. A minor negative is an apparent conscious choice to dial back on seafood, allowing the buffet to offer high-quality items in the other areas (kind of like managing a salary cap in sports). Show the lowest-level casino players card for a $2 discount on all meals.

The Feast (Palace Station)
(702) 367-2411

Only a few months after the debut of the Palms' A.Y.C.E., Palace Station upped the bar with its revamped Feast. Relocated on the main floor in a sparkling new space, this is another small-plates format with choice and quality equal to that of the Palms, while priced $2-$5 lower across the board. It's an interesting full-circle move, given that the whole evolution of the Las Vegas buffet began 30 years ago when Palace Station introduced the "action" concept with the original Feast Buffet. Further distinguishing this excellent value play, it offers the city's only graveyard buffet, meaning you can eat there all hours except 9 p.m. to midnight.

Additional Recommendations

SLIDERS AT B.B.D.'s

BURGERS

b.B.d.'s (Essential 52: see page 26)

Bobby's Burger Palace (The Shops at Crystals)
(702) 598-0191

Bobby Flay's burgers trump anything he's doing at Mesa Grill, although the burger there is also one of Vegas' best.

Burger Bar (Mandalay Place)
(702) 632-9364

Hubert Keller was the first fancy chef to bring a burger concept to Las Vegas and his are still some of the best.

Carson Kitchen (Essential 52: see page 30)

Kerry Simon's butter burger is a legacy that does his memory proud.

CUT (Essential 52: see page 36)

Get the sliders at the bar.

Delmonico Steakhouse (see page 163)

Unlike most steakhouses, it's open for lunch and the burger is the thing to get with a nice glass of vin rouge.

Fatburger (multiple locations)
6775 W. Flamingo Road
(702) 889-9009

Next to Smashburger, this is my favorite franchised meat patty on a bun.

Fat Choy Restaurant (Eureka Casino)
(702) 794-0829

Sheridan Su's fusion burger is a piled-high delight.

Fleur by Hubert Keller (Mandalay Place)
(702) 632-9400

When a fine French chef does a bison burger like this one, we pay attention.

Fukuburger
3429 S. Jones Boulevard
(702) 262-6995

They put everything but the kitchen sink on these pan-Pacific patties, and if that's your thing, have at it.

Gordon Ramsay BurGR (Planet Hollywood)
(702) 785-5462

This is actually my favorite of the bombastic Brit's four Vegas eateries. And shhhhhh … don't tell anyone, but the hot dogs are just as good as the burgers.

Holsteins Shakes and Buns (Cosmopolitan)
(702) 698-7940

Perfect for when your nightclub buzz is wearing off at the Cosmo.

In-N-Out Burger
(multiple locations)
4888 Dean Martin Drive
(702) 768-1000

Classics never go out of style. Nor does this "secret menu." Do you get yours "animal style"?

NOM NOM BURGER AT HOLSTEINS SHAKES AND BUNS

Marché Bacchus (Essential 52: see page 76)

A serious burger in a stunning setting.

John Curtas

NoMad Bar (NoMad Hotel)
(833) 706-6623

This New York import might make the best hamburger and hot dog in America.

Shake Shack
(multiple locations)
New York-New York
(725) 222-6730

BURGER AT NOMAD BAR

Danny Meyer took this concept public to great acclaim … on Wall Street, no less. Aficionados know his is but a tepid ode to In-N-Out, at a substantially higher price. Still, people line up for them, so who am I to argue?

Smashburger (multiple locations)
smashburger.com

Everything is made fresh, so it's slower than the usual fast-food, but the taste is worth the wait. Avoid the Caesars' food court Smashburger, whose prices are too dear.

Steak & Shake (South Point)
(702) 796-7111

I've been eating Steak & Shake burgers since I was six. These new franchises try to re-capture the glory of smashed grilled burgers, skinny fries, and Chili Macs from the '60s, but lack the proper seasoning that comes with great memories.

Stripburger (Fashion Show Mall)
(702) 737-8747

Decent burgers and shakes; great people-watching.

White Castle (2 locations)
Casino Royale / 3411 S. Las Vegas Boulevard
(702) 227-8531 / (702) 227-8531

The original sliders are now on the Strip, muting the munchies and helping to halt hangovers at 4 a.m.

Additional Recommendations

COOKIE ASSORTMENT AT LULU'S BREAD AND BREAKFAST

DESSERTS

Allegro (see "Close, But No Cigar" page 129)
(702) 770-2040

Leave the gun, eat the cannoli!

Carson Kitchen (Essential 52: see page 30)

The desserts change seasonally and never more than a few are on the menu, but your table will be fighting for the last bite.

Chef Flemming's Bake Shop
7 S. Water Street B & C, Henderson
(702) 566-6500

There are precious few reasons ever to venture to downtown Henderson, least of all to eat, but this little shop is a gem and worth the journey.

Delmonico Steakhouse (see page 163)

Steakhouse dessert used to be nothing but cheesecake and peach melba. Not so at Delmonico, where Diane Wong knows how to keep purists and fussy foodies alike satisfied.

Gelato di Milano
4950 S. Rainbow Boulevard, #140
(702) 888-1133

Simple unpretentious shop that has the best gelato in town, period. One lick and you'll swear you're in Italy.

Hexx Kitchen + Bar (Paris Las Vegas)
(702) 331-5100

Carol Garcia does bean-to-bar chocolate on a par with anything you'll find on either coast, and the rest of her sweets and shakes ain't too shabby either.

Lulu's Bread & Breakfast
6720 Sky Pointe Drive
(702) 437-5858

Big, fat, flaky, fruity pastries on the north side of town, with some interesting fresh-baked breads to take home with you, too.

Luv-It Frozen Custard
505 E. Oakey Boulevard
(702) 384-6452

A must-do for some, I think this place is now coasting on its reputation.

Mothership Coffee Roasters
2708 N. Green Valley Parkway, Henderson
(702) 456-1869

Single-origin cold-brewed coffee on tap is complemented by pastries made using whole wheat flour all the way from Washington state.

Pinkbox Doughnuts
9435 W. Tropicana Avenue
(702) 222-3370

Family owned and operated and completely fantastic.

Sweets Raku
(Essential 52: see page 98)

Twist
(Essential 52: see page 116)

RIBBON DONUT AT PINKBOX DOUGHNUTS

Vivian Chang creates an array of sweets that dazzle and perplex as only Gagnaire can.

Yardbird Southern Table & Bar (Venetian)
(702) 297-6541

Lots of Southern-style fried, baked, and whipped goodness.

John Curtas

ITALIAN

Ada's (Tivoli Village)
410 S. Rampart, #120
(702) 463-7433

James Trees' offshoot of
Esther's Kitchen is the only
reason to eat at Tivoli Village.
It stands out in this overblown,
under-performing, shopping
center like an island of quality amidst a sea of mediocrity.
Save room for ice cream.

SPAGHETTI CON POLPETTE AT ADA'S

Allegro
(see "Close, But No Cigar" page 129)

Located in the often overly opulent Wynn, this is an approachable
place for ravioli with dandelion greens and pancetta. Reasonably
priced for the venue.

Ambra Italian Kitchen + Bar (MGM Grand)
(702) 891-7600

Passels of pulchritudinous pasta, albeit in a restaurant the size of
an airplane hangar.

Carbone (see "Close, But No Cigar" page 129)

Waiters in velvet jackets. Veal marsala the size of a hubcap. Settle
in! Bring money.

Casa di Amore
2850 E. Tropicana Avenue
(702) 433-4967

Old Vegas east of the Strip. Chow on cioppino and osso buco
while being entertained by live Rat Pack-style singers. Plus, free
shuttles from the Strip. Dino and Sammy would approve.

Cucina by Wolfgang Puck (The Shops at Crystals)
(702) 238-1000

The Wolf's fancy pies include tomatoey margherita and several wood-fired meat-laden combos.

Esther's Kitchen (Essential 52: see page 48)

Ferraro's Italian Restaurant & Wine Bar (Essential 52: see page 52)

Gino Ferraro has one of the best Italian wine lists in the city, and runs that rarest of creatures: a venerable Italian restaurant that seems to get better every year.

La Strega
3555 S. Town Center Drive, #105
(702) 722 -2099

Super-slick Italian that's not as sophisticated as it thinks it is. Ignore the starters and clichés (octopus, shishito peppers, so-so salads) and concentrate on Gina Marinelli's pastas, pizzas, and proteins. Wonderful short wine list.

Locale Italian Kitchen
7995 Blue Diamond Road, #106
(702) 330-0404

Along with La Strega and Ada's, Locale radically upped Las Vegas' neighborhood-Italian food game over the past year. La Strega gets the nod for its bright and friendly decor, but the food is better here. Whether it's good enough to entice exec chef Nicole Brisson's fans to this remote location remains to be seen.

John Curtas

Manzo (Park MGM)
(702) 730-7617

A great Italian restaurant that also happens to be a great steak-house. Or is it the other way around? Nice Italian wine list too.

Nora's Italian Cuisine
5780 W. Flamingo Road
(702) 873-8990

A big menu packed with every conceivable variation on pastas, pizzas, and parmigianas. Recently built its own new building with a sparkling bar, patio dining, and a bocce ball court.

CLAMS AT NORA'S ITALIAN CUISINE

Pasta Shop Ristorante & Art Gallery
2525 W. Horizon Ridge Parkway, Henderson
(702) 451-1893

A funky little nook in the southern 'burbs. The food here isn't that bad … but it's not that good either.

Rao's (Caesars Palace)
(702) 731-7267

Sit down for serious dining with Uncle Vincent's lemon chicken, spicy meatballs, and eggplant Parmesan. After dinner, play bocce ball in the heart of the Caesars Palace pool complex.

Italian (Pizza)

Amore Taste of Chicago
3945 S. Durango Drive, #A8
(702) 562-9000

They make an excellent crusty deep-dish tomato pie, if you're into that sort of thing.

Brooksy's Bar and Grill
9295 W. Flamingo Road
(702) 562-2050

Best veggie pies in town. Eat 'em while watching live hockey in the attached ice rink.

Dom DeMarco's Pizzeria & Bar
9785 W. Charleston Boulevard
(702) 570-7000

Nestled in tony Summerlin, Dom's uses the recipes from Brooklyn's famous DiFara Pizza and the pies are amazing (so is the happy hour). President Obama ordered dozens of pizzas delivered during an overnight Vegas stay.

Evel Pie (see page 156)

The best New York slice in Sin City is on East Fremont Street.

Good Pie (see page 156)

Brooklyn style pizza spot offering authentic back-East deck-oven pies. When only a New York slice will do.

Grimaldi's (several locations)
Palazzo Hotel-Casino
(702) 754-3448

Coal-fired brick ovens—just like the Brooklyn original.

Metro Pizza (multiple locations)
4001 S. Decatur Boulevard
(702) 362-7896

The granddaddy of Vegas pizza joints still turns out killer pies.

Pizza Rock (2 locations)
Downtown Grand / Green Valley Ranch
(702) 385-0838 / (702) 616-2996

A dozen different categories of pizza, including Napoletana, Romana, Sicilian, Classic Italian, New York, New Haven, and Chicago. If you can't find something you like here, you should stop eating pizza.

John Curtas

Pizzeria Monzu (Essential 52: see page 96)

Pop Up Pizza (see page 158)

Great slices are sometimes found in unlikely places.

Secret Pizza (Comospolitan)
(702) 698-7860

New York thin-and-crispy slices and pies available in a hidden nook (follow the vintage record-album covers down the long hallway) on the second floor of Cosmo.

Settebello Pizzeria Napoletana (2 locations)
9350 W. Sahara Avenue, #170
140 S. Green Valley Parkway, Henderson
(702) 901-4877 / (702) 222-3556

This is the king of pizzerias, thanks to old-world Neapolitan standards, top-quality ingredients, and the blistering-hot wood-burning ovens.

CAPRESE SALAD AT GRIMALDI'S

Additional Recommendations

AL PASTOR TACOS AT BORDER GRILL

MEXICAN

Border Grill (Mandalay Bay)
(702) 632-7403

The best Mexican restaurant in town to be found in a casino. The weekend brunch is a banger.

China Poblano (Cosmopolitan)
(702) 698-7900

Don't let the China-meets-Mexico vibe fool you: Everything, from the cochinita (Yucatan-style) barbecue pork tacos to the pozole rojo soup, is some of the best you will ever taste.

El Menudazo
3100 E. Lake Mead Boulevard, #18, North Las Vegas
(702) 944-9706

Way out of the way, up in the heart of North Las Vegas, where most gringos fear to tread. My advice: Go for lunch and get a huge bowl of pozole.

Frijoles & Frescas Grilled Tacos (multiple locations)
4811 S. Rainbow Boulevard
(702) 483-5399

Good, not great, but the frescas are fun and the lines are out the door.

KoMex Fusion Express
633 N. Decatur Boulevard #H
(702) 646-1612

Korea-meets-Mexico-fusion-fun, or put another way: bulgogi meets the burrito. There's nothing subtle about this food, but it's wildly and inexplicably popular with a certain sort of chowhound.

FUSION FLAUTAS AT KOMEX FUSION EXPRESS

Additional Recommendations

Lindo Michoacan (multiple "Michoacan" locations)
2655 E. Desert Inn Road
(702) 735-6828

Fresh tortillas, amazing margaritas, and lots of lengua (tongue) keep me coming back to the original on East Desert Inn. The offshoots around town aren't nearly as good.

Los Molcajetes
1553 N. Eastern Avenue
(702) 633-7595

Another out-of-the-way place on the Las Vegas/North Las Vegas border, with large volcanic molcajetes (thick, round, stone mortars) holding all sorts of spicy stews. Don't speak English? No problem, since few others in the joint do either. The servers, however, are very sweet and helpful to us *gueros*.

Serrano's Mexican Food
136 S. Rainbow Boulevard
(702) 243-4552

A homey little place in a forlorn shopping center with handmade food far above your usual mediocre Mex. Wonderful menudo, burritos, nachos, and flan, all made according to the family's recipes. It took me 14 years to discover this place; you shouldn't wait so long.

Tres Cazuelas Artisanal Latin Cuisine
3555 Spring Mountain Road, #35
(702) 370-0751

The name's translation, "Three Pots," also signifies three cuisines, as owner Angelo Reyes brings the best of Mexico, Spain, and South America to your table. The moles are a dream, the tortillas addictive, and the tapas lunch a genuine bargain. Highly seasoned in-your-face flavors punctuate some of the most interesting dishes in town. The oddball location is actually quite convenient, right at the start of Chinatown. A beautiful hidden little gem.

TAPAS AT TRES CAZUELAS ARTISANAL LATIN CUISINE

John Curtas

Mexican (Tacos)

Abuela's Tacos
4225 E. Sahara Avenue
(702) 431-0284

The house-made tortillas alone are worth the trip.

El Birotazo
4262 E. Charleston Boulevard
(702) 888-0858

The tortas ahogadas (served on substantial French bread) are the Guadalajaran specialties here. You'll be the only gringo in the joint, but the service is fast and friendly and those sandwiches and salsas are serious. One of the best holes-in-the-wall in Las Vegas.

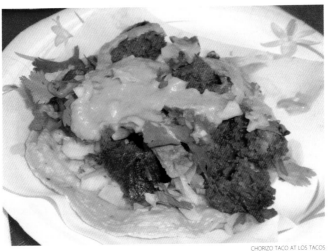

CHORIZO TACO AT LOS TACOS

Los Tacos (2 locations)
1710 E. Charleston Boulevard / 4001 W. Sahara Avenue
(702) 471-7447 / (702) 252-0100

Santos Guisados Tacos & Beer (see page 158)

The best tacos in town, period. Don't even think of arguing with me about this.

Additional Recommendations

Sin Frontera Tacos
4016 N. Tenaya Way
(702) 866-0080

The second-best tacos I had this year were way up in the northwest part of town. They were more than worth the 13-mile jaunt from my house.

Tacos El Compita (2 locations)
6118 W. Charleston B oulevard / 7622 Westcliff Drive
(702) 878-0008 / (702) 319-8283

Better than most, not as good as others.

Tacos El Gordo (multiple locations)
3049 S. Las Vegas Boulevard
(702) 929-2249

An authentic taqueria with the language barrier to prove it. Get in line and point and prepare to be impressed.

Tacos Mexico (multiple locations)
1800 S. Las Vegas Boulevard
(702) 444-2288

For when you really really need a taco at 2 a.m.

Taqueria El Buen Pastor (multiple locations)
301 S. Decatur Boulevard
(702) 432-5515

Guadalajara street tacos to beat the band. Look for the taco wagon at the corner of Bonanza and Las Vegas Boulevard to nab some righteous al pastor beauties, 24/7.

John Curtas

SUSHI

Hiroyoshi Japanese Cuisine (see "Close, But No Cigar" page 129)

Kabuto (Essential 52: see page 60)

Kaiseki Yuzu (Essential 52: see page 62)

Gorgeous, authentic omakase and kaiseki meals served to a neighborhood that has no idea how great the food is.

Naked Fish's Sushi & Grill
3945 S. Durango Drive, #A6
(702) 228-8856

SUSHI SAMPLER AT NAKED FISH'S SUSHI & GRILL

Westside hang where you're apt to see a television poker pro or two around World Series of Poker time. Check the blackboard for the live shrimp (when it's in season).

Soho Japanese Restaurant
(see page 147)

Westside sleeper, building a big reputation with sushi aficionados.

Sushi Fever
7985 W. Sahara Avenue, #105
(702) 838-2927

For the California-roll lover in you.

Yellowtail Japanese Restaurant & Lounge (Bellagio)
(702) 730-3900

Inventive fish. Fabulous sake list.

Yui Edomae Sushi (Essential 52: see page 124)

JIDORI CHICKEN AT ALDER & BIRCH

LOCAL FAVORITES

CHEAP EATS

Alder & Birch (The Orleans Hotel & Casino)
(702) 365-7111

This shiny steak-centric eatery in a popular off-Strip casino features handsome modern design reminiscent of something in Seattle or San Francisco. Dine on Wagyu beef or Jidori chicken here quite more affordably than two miles east on Las Vegas Boulevard.

Big Wong (see page 141)

It's located in a strip mall with some of our priciest eateries, but everything here—noodle soups, curries, shrimp wontons—is priced below $10. The jalapeño chicken wings are insane!

Casa Don Juan
(see page 155)

STEAK CARNE ASADA AT CASA DON JUAN

Getting a seat in this place is nearly impossible on weekends. Nonetheless, it's a rite of passage for southern Nevadans.

Doña Maria Tamales Restaurant (2 locations)
910 S. Las Vegas Boulevard / 3205 N. Tenaya Way
(702) 382-6538 / (702) 656-1600

A pilgrimage place for Las Vegans of all stripes for corn-husked masa packets.

Fat Choy Restaurant (see page 175)

A casino diner that serves the unexpected—e.g., steamed bao and duck leg confit on white Jasmine rice, alongside short-rib grilled cheese and kalbi steak & eggs. Expect to be impressed.

Fat Greek Mediterranean Bistro
4001 S. Decatur Boulevard, #34
(702) 222-0666

Family-owned hot spot for lunch, TFG serves authentic Greek/Armenian fare made from scratch. Leave room for the awesome desserts and pastries.

Flock & Fowl
150 N. Las Vegas Boulevard, #100
(702) 272-2222

Poached chicken, shmaltz rice, broth, and dips. So simple, but there's a reason why it's one of the most popular dishes in Asia. Good chicken wings and bombastic bao.

Forte European Tapas Bar & Bistro
4180 S. Rainbow Boulevard
(702) 220-3876

This Bulgarian-Armenian-Hungarian-Greek-Russian-Spanish tapas bar has been a hit with foodies and Vegas' Central European community since day one. Don't miss the flavored vodkas or a chat with owner Nina Manchev.

HOME-MADE PICKLED VEGGIES AND A TOAST AT FORTE EUROPEAN TAPAS BAR & BISTRO

John Curtas

Harrie's Bagelmania
855 E. Twain Avenue, #120
(702) 369-3322

Bagels, smoked fish, bountiful breakfasts, and big deli sandwiches till closing at 3 p.m.

Honey Salt
1031 S. Rampart Boulevard
(702) 445-6100

For ladies who lunch and brunch. A tough ticket on weekends, for good reason.

Kitchen Table
1716 W. Horizon Ridge Parkway, #100
(702) 478-4782

Somewhat remotely located near the edge of Henderson, this modernistic kitchen serves upscale breakfasts and lunches daily inside or on the patio.

Lulu's Bread & Breakfast (see page 180)

In other cities across the western U.S., eateries like Lulu's are the norm. In Las Vegas, it stands out for all the morning and midday reasons. The perfect stop on the way to hiking at Mt. Charleston.

M&M Soul Food Café
2211 S. Las Vegas Boulevard
(702) 478-5767

This nondescript lunch counter puts forth superb fried chicken and waffles, cornbread, collard greens, corned-beef hash, and decent-enough barbecued ribs to almost make you think you're in Mississippi.

New York Bagel N Bakery
840 S. Rancho Drive
(702) 258-7400

The Italian sweets are superb and the bagels are even better.

Nora's Italian Cuisine (see page 183)

This long-operating local fave serves large portions off a big menu with almost nothing priced at more than $20. In a new (and bigger) location, it's now an after-work hotspot.

Norm's Diner (2 locations)
3945 S. Durango Drive, #A1 / 35 S. Gibson Road, Henderson
(702) 431-3447 / (702) 333-0014

Possibly the largest breakfast menu in town, from omelets and Benedicts to pancakes and frittatas—even an off-menu creamed chipped beef on toast. Bring your pooch and dine on the dog-friendly patio.

Other Mama (Essential 52: see page 90)

Paymon's Mediterranean Café & Lounge (multiple locations)
8955 S. Eastern Avenue / 8380 W. Sahara Avenue
(702) 731-6030

Barely average Mediterranean fare, but the extended-happy hour prices have made these a favorite among the undiscerning.

Perú Chicken Rotisserie (2 locations)
2055 E. Tropicana / 3886 W. Sahara Avenue
(702) 732-0079 / (702) 982-0073

The rotisserie chicken is good, but the prize here is the ceviche, made with chunks of "premier" sea bass and served with potato, corn, and toasted corn on the side.

Roma Deli & Restaurant
5755 W. Spring Mountain Road
(702) 871-5577

This bustling Italian restaurant, deli, and bakery is the real deal for lunch or dinner. Try a hot or cold sub on their fresh-baked bread. Warning: The cookies are addictive.

LOMO SALTADO AT PERÚ CHICKEN ROTISSERIE

John Curtas

Shiraz Indian & Mediterranean Cuisine
2575 S. Decatur Boulevard
(702) 870-0680

A huge menu of Middle Eastern, Persian, and Indian fare that the kitchen executes well across the continent. For our money, though, the rice dishes of Persia (biryani) are where things really shine.

Sin City Smokers Barbecue & Catering
2861 N. Green Valley Parkway, Henderson
(702) 823-5605

Las Vegas is where barbecue goes to die. Whenever good 'cue has come to these parts, it hasn't lasted. The shitty stuff hangs around forever. SCS just may buck that trend, with smoked meats and sides that are seriously succulent.

SPICY PULLED PORK AT SIN CITY SMOKERS

Tap House
5589 W. Charleston Boulevard
(702) 870-2111

Famed for its pizza and wings (half-price late nights and all weekend). Monday's free open-mic sessions pack the back room with aging mobsters and their dolled-up dames—real-life time traveling!

Todd's Unique Dining
4350 E. Sunset Road, Henderson
(702) 259-8633

Todd Clore is at the stoves every night, keeping Henderson well-fed and giving me a reason to travel there.

Valencian Gold
7960 S. Rainbow Boulevard, #8000A
(702) 776-7707

Two amigos who trained in Spain bring impeccable paella to an area (South Rainbow Boulevard) that's getting much tastier. Authentic, fresh, and criminally cheap.

Vintner Grill
10100 W. Charleston Boulevard, #150
(702) 214-5590

Nothing about this place is as good as its reputation.

Zaytoon Market & Restaurant
3655 S. Durango Drive, #11-14
(702) 685-1875

Located on the west side, Zaytoon is an in-the-know place for Persian cuisine. The hummus is among the best in town.

BEEF KOOBIDEH AND CHICKEN KABOB AT ZAYTOON MARKET & RESTAURANT

John Curtas

CLASSIC VEGAS

Bootlegger Italian Bistro
7700 S. Las Vegas Boulevard
(702) 736-4939

Former Strip singer and lieutenant governor Lorraine Hunt's family has owned the Bootlegger since 1949. It's changed locations over the years, but it still relies on the same tried-and-true family recipes. And you never know what Strip performers might stop by late at night to work out some new material on the dining-room stage, which, if you're lucky, will distract you from the food.

Chicago Joe's Restaurant
820 S. 4th Street
(702) 382-5637

It's a downtown institution, but old-time fare like minestrone soup and spaghetti and meatballs is the best you can hope for and all you'll get.

Golden Steer Steakhouse
308 W. Sahara Avenue
(702) 384-4470

With a tuxedoed maître d', oversized booths dedicated to the celebrities that once frequented them, and cowboy art and memorabilia on the walls, a meal at the Golden Steer is a walk back through its 60-year history. The Rat Packers all ate here (at booths named after them) and the food hasn't aged as well as they have.

Hitchin' Post Saloon and Steakhouse
3650 N. Las Vegas Boulevard
(702) 644-1220

A classic value steakhouse located on the far north end of Las Vegas Boulevard with complete steak dinners priced under $20. Eat in the little enclosed steak room, at the bar, or on the outside patio next to a horseshoe pit.

12-OZ RIB EYE AT HITCHIN' POST SALOON

Additional Recommendations

Hugo's Cellar (Four Queens)
(702) 385-4011

Ladies are presented with a rose as they enter this fine-dining restaurant in the basement of the Four Queens, and after your meal you get a selection of chocolate-dipped figs, apricots, and strawberries. In between, there's attentive tableside service and butter hand-crafted into the shape of a rose. Just like in 1978. Just like an era we'd all like to forget.

Italian-American Club Restaurant
2333 E. Sahara Avenue
(702) 457-3866

Operating since 1961, the IAC was originally a men's social club boasting a membership that included Frank Sinatra, along with several other showbiz and "sporting" types. Those kinds of guys still come around, but it's mostly for the pasta and live entertainment.

Lawry's The Prime Rib

Though born in L.A. and not a true Vegas original, it's been here long enough to be vibrantly vintage. It does perfect prime rib and Yorkshire pudding in a clubby timeless setting.

Michael's Gourmet Room (South Point)
(702) 796-7111

It's totally overpriced, so try to get a casino comp. Try the veal Française and the Caesar salad, mixed tableside, and then try to stifle a yawn, and try to stifle a heart attack when you get the bill.

Mt. Charleston Lodge
5375 Kyle Canyon Road
(702) 872-5408

Escape the heat by driving up to Mt. Charleston Lodge for the elk, buffalo, and traditional burgers. Bring your pooch and eat on the doggie deck (just don't sit next to me).

MOUNTAIN CHILI, FRIED BUFFALO CAULIFLOWER,
BUFFALO BURGER AND FRIES AT MT. CHARLESTON LODGE

John Curtas

BROCCOLI & CHEESE OMELET AT OMELET HOUSE

Omelet House (multiple locations)
2160 W. Charleston
(702) 384-6868

A long-time locals fave, a booth is reserved for famous former Mayor Oscar Goodman and his wife Carolyn, the current mayor.

Pamplemousse Le Restaurant
400 E. Sahara Avenue
(702) 733-2066

A Gallic joint named by crooner Bobby Darin that somehow hasn't given up the ghost, and somehow convinces gullible tourists to pay for their meal.

Peppermill Restaurant and Fireside Lounge
2985 S. Las Vegas Boulevard
(702) 735-7635

Visiting the Peppermill at night, basking in its neon glow and getting buzzed, is a locals' rite of passage.

Piero's Italian Cuisine
355 Convention Center Drive
(702) 369-2305

A certain type of Old Vegas lounge lizard will tell you Piero's is the best Italian restaurant in town. They tend to be related to the New Vegas lounge lizards who say the same thing about Panevino.

Additional Recommendations

Pioneer Saloon
310 NV-161, Goodsprings
(702) 874-9362

A 45-minute drive southwest of Vegas brings you to the unmistakable Pioneer Saloon in the wilds of the Mojave Desert. It's great, especially when there's live music. Try the Ghost BBQ Burger (fired with

GHOST BURGER AT PIONEER SALOON

the magma-like Bhut jolokia pepper) and a cold beevo, or get caveman fancy with a huge tomahawk rib eye steak for two. It's been here since 1913. Bikers and photographers love this place.

The Bagel Café
301 N. Buffalo Drive
(702) 255-3444

Nevada movers and shakers, plus many others, flock here for big breakfasts, bialys, and soup straight off the Sysco truck.

Top of Binion's Steakhouse (Binion's Gambling Hall)
(702) 382-1600

Venture to the 24th floor of the namesake downtown casino to enjoy chicken-fried lobster and a glass of vino with one of the best views in town.

Vickie's Diner
1700 S. Las Vegas Boulevard
(702) 444-4459

Known for decades as White Cross Drugs, this diner, located between the north end of the Strip and downtown, is still serving breakfasts, burgers, and more, 24/7.

John Curtas

WHAT'S FOR LUNCH?

Is a proper sit-down lunch in Las Vegas as obsolete as Wayne Newton? Well, yes and no.

Las Vegas is a different kettle of fish from other gastronomic destinations. Here, the tens of thousands of visitors are either sleeping, shopping, too hung over to be bothered, or roaming a convention hall. Because of this, many of our best restaurants are closed for lunch and the midday pickings are slim—unless you're in the right hotel, close to downtown, or within a chopstick or two of Chinatown.

But if you're looking for a good lunch, you've come to the right place, pilgrim. For the sake of this chapter, I'm dividing these meals into two categories: power lunches and foodie favorites. The first is for those quiet business meetings that are always more digestible in a nice setting. The second consist of establishments (some more exotic than others) where the food takes precedence over the décor. Put another way: The first group is where I go for my big-deal meals, the second where I eat every day when the sun is highest in the sky.

Power Lunching

Capital Grill (Fashion Show Mall)
(702) 932-6631

A chain steakhouse, but a great one, with white tablecloths, good service, and nice lunch specials.

Cipriani (Essential 52: see page 34)

The day it opened, it was the place to go for meetings or just munching on some of the best pastas in town.

TORTELLINI PANNA PISELLI E PROSCIUTTO
AT CIPRIANI

Additional Recommendations

Delmonico Steakhouse (see page 163)

Great steaks, luxurious surroundings, an awesome burger, and a world-beating wine list make for a hushed elegant midday repast. It's never crowded and the food tastes the same as dinner ... only the prices are easier to swallow.

Eiffel Tower Restaurant (see page 167)

Dinner is packed with young couples celebrating their starter marriages. Lunch is calmer and less delusional.

Estiatorio Milos Cosmopolitan (Essential 52: see page 50)

Fresh-off-the-boat fish that doesn't cost a fortune between 11:30 a.m. and 3 p.m., as long as you stick to the lunch specials. Always packed.

Ferraro's Italian Restaurant & Wine Bar
(Essential 52: see page 52)

Movers and shakers aplenty populate these tables at noon. Most of them are too busy with business to notice how good the food is.

RED SNAPPER AT ESTIATORIO MILOS

Marché Bacchus (Essential 52: see page 76)

Al fresco dining so nice, you're liable to forget yourself and spend the afternoon drinking bottle after bottle from its wonderful wine list. But enough about me.

Morel's Steakhouse & Bistro (see page 131)
(702) 607-6333

Morel's flies under the radar, but it's my first choice when a group of hungry guys asks me where they should chow down.

John Curtas

Old Soul (Essential 52: see page 88)

Quiet, secluded, a bit dark, and very cozy, the perfect place to conduct a hush-hush meeting (or an affair), although some of us prefer to concentrate on Natalie Young's fried oysters and superlative soups.

Spago (Essential 52: see page 106)

Beautiful setting, fabulous food, lots of dudes in suits.

Top of the World Restaurant & Lounge (The Strat)
(702) 380-7777

Way too touristy for anyone who isn't a tourist and the food isn't in the same league, but the view is spectacular.

Veranda (Four Seasons)
(702) 632-5121

A south Strip staple where the elite meet to eat.

Foodie Favorites

7th & Carson (see page 155)

New chef Sammy DeMarco is set to bring this place into the spotlight.

Carson Kitchen (Essential 52: see page 30)

This downtown pioneer hasn't lost its fastball.

China Mama (Essential 52: see page 32)

QUINOA SALAD WITH BLT SANDWICH AT 7TH & CARSON

A steamer full of xiao long bao is just about the perfect noontime nosh.

EATT Gourmet Bistro (Essential 52: see page 42)

Shhhh! Don't tell anyone, but in some ways I prefer the lighter healthier fare here to that at its fancier sibling Partage.

Esther's Kitchen (Essential 52: see page 48)

Downtown's favorite lunch spot is too loud at peak times, so go after the gold rush … around 1 p.m.

Jaleo (Essential 52: see page 56)

I sometimes forget Jaleo is open for lunch. That's a good thing; otherwise, I'd be here all the time.

Lotus of Siam (Essential 52: see page 72)

It's easier to get a table at lunch, before the FOMO crowd has descended. (For you landlubbers, that means "fear of missing out.")

Mabel's BBQ (Essential 52: see page 74)

More relaxed at lunch, which also gives you the rest of the day to digest those ginormous platters of smoked meat.

John Curtas

Mon Ami Gabi (see page 168)

It's a pain in the ass to get to (unless you're staying on the Strip), but the steak frites and people-watching are worth the trip.

New Asian BBQ Tan Tung Ky (see page 142)

My new go-to for superior dim sum on Spring Mountain Road.

Santos Guisados Tacos & Beer (see page 158)

Best. Tacos. In. Town. Why do I have to keep telling you these things?

Shang Artisan Noodle (see page 143)

Hand-pulled noodles straight from Taiwan, by way of UNLV (the owner is a graduate).

The Goodwich (see page 158)

Sometimes, only one of these hand-tooled sandwiches will do.

Tres Cazuelas Artisanal Latin Cuisine (see page 188)

The newest spot on my lunch rotation; Angelo Reyes seamlessly combines Latino cuisines in a tiny restaurant that punches way above its weight.

Additional Recommendations

FIREPIT LOUNGE AT PEPPERMILL

LATE NIGHT

The best place to research hundreds of late-night Vegas restaurants is LasVegasAdvisor.com; in the top navigation menu, hover over Eat, then click on Restaurants. On the Restaurants landing page, click on Advanced Restaurant Search, then select the Late Night box near the top. Note that almost all the casino coffee shops and many of the noodle bars are open with 24 hours or into the wee hours. Here are some of the most popular, convenient, and best late-night eateries.

American Coney Island (the D)
(702) 388-2120

For exactly 100 years, these Dearborn Sausage-brand hot dogs, topped with fine mustard, sweet chopped onions, and a secret family-recipe chili sauce, have been a favorite of Detroiters. The location at the D is this stand's first location outside Michigan. Open 24 hours daily.

Bootlegger Italian Bistro (see page 199)

Open 24 hours daily.

Capriotti's Sandwich Shop (multiple locations)
4480 Paradise Road
(702) 736-6166

The one Capriotti's that's open day and night is convenient to the partyers at the Hard Rock.

Casa di Amore (see page 181)

Open Wed.-Mon. until 5 a.m.

Hash House A Go-Go (LINQ)
(702) 254-4646

Monster portions of oversized pancakes, breakfast scrambles, hashes, Benedicts, and other breakfasts have given this chain an almost cult following; they also serve a casual lunch and dinner. Open daily 24 hours.

Additional Recommendations

Hexx Kitchen + Bar (see page 179)

Centrally located with a recommendable menu, Hexx is open 24 hours a day. The patio generally closes at midnight, but that that can vary, depending on the weather. If it's open and warm out, it's a fine people-watching opportunity.

Honey Pig (see page 149)

Open daily 24 hours.

Krung Siam Thai (see page 151)

Open daily until 5:30 a.m.

Musashi Japanese Steakhouse
3900 Paradise Road
(702) 735-4744

Sushi, teppanyaki, and a late-night happy hour are the big draws here. Open daily until 4 a.m.

Peppermill Restaurant (see page 201)

Coffee-shop fare in a veteran of decades on the Strip. Open daily 24 hours.

Ping Pang Pong (see page 143)

Open daily until 3 a.m.

Pin-Up Pizza (Planet Hollywood)
(702) 785-5888

Each New York thin-crust slice is the size of 2-1/2 regular slices at less than twice the price. Open daily until 4 a.m.

Pizzeria Monzu (Essential 52: see page 96)

Raku (Essential 52: see page 98)

This place typically bustles right up until the final seating. Open daily until 2 a.m.

Secret Pizza (see page 185)

Open daily until 5 a.m.

ALBUM-COVER-LINED HALLWAY LEADING TO SECRET PIZZA AT COSMO

Vickie's Diner (see page 202)

This is the oldest diner in Las Vegas, at the same location as when it was Tiffany's, the counter at the defunct White Cross Drugs. A classic, serving three meals, all available 24/7/365.

White Castle (see page 177)

In case of a center Strip emergency where you must have food! now!, you can get some fast-food (and nostalgic) sliders at the 24/7 White Castles next to Casino Royale, downtown, and Terrible's Roadhouse in Jean. A new location is opening on Paradise Road.

Wolfgang Puck Bar & Grill (MGM Grand)
(702) 891-3000

This shrine to classic California cuisine opens wide onto the casino floor, so it's lively and busy, even as the sun is coming up. Open Wed.-Sun., until 6 a.m.

Additional Recommendations

PEOPLE/
CELEBRITY WATCHING

Andiamo Steakhouse (the D)
(702) 388-2400

The D's Italian steakhouse has proven to be a hit with the famous friends of flamboyant casino owner Derek Stevens, including stars of UFC, WWE, and NASCAR and the casts of TV's "Pawn Stars" and "Sons of Anarchy."

"PAWN STARS" COREY HARRISON AT ANDIAMO STEAKHOUSE

Bazaar Meat
(Essential 52: see page 24)

"This is why you are here!" chef José Andrés—who eats whatever makes him "feel like a lion"—roars from the menu, but there are no human sacrifices of starlets or socialites in the fire pit and this restaurant's vibe is designed to be as playful as the cuisine and its creator.

Border Grill (see page 187)

Patio views of the famous Lazy River at Mandalay Beach or of the hordes enjoying some high-end retail therapy in the Forum Shops—take your pick from the "Too Hot Tamales'" two Vegas locations, both of which offer plenty of people-watching potential from a relaxed vantage point.

CRUSH (MGM Grand)

If you want to catch Rick Moonen nibbling on gnocchi, George Strait savoring a steak, Dita Von Teese dining on a date & artichoke flatbread, or Bruce Buffer toying with Tuna 2 Ways, this place is your best bet to do it.

Additional Recommendations

CUT (Essential 52: see page 36)

Proprietor Wolfgang Puck knows the whole of Hollywood and many of his famous fans choose to get their steak fix here when slumming in Vegas.

Hexx Kitchen + Bar (see page 179)

The new hangout for sweet-toothed celebs—from rapper 50 Cent to Playmate Kennedy Summers—is also giving neighbor Mon Ami Gabi a run for its money, with its matching patio views of the passing hoi polloi on Las Vegas Boulevard.

La Cave (Wynn Las Vegas)

Katy Perry, Amber Rose, Troy Aikman, Neil Patrick Harris, Yeardley Smith, Michael McDonald, Patrick Monahan, Sebastian Maniscalco, Kenny Mayne, Nick Cannon, Akon—it would probably be quicker to list the celebrities who haven't yet been spotted at this place.

STEPHANIE PRATT & NOLE MARIN AT LAVO

LAVO Italian Restaurant (Palazzo)
(702) 791-1800

This perennially popular "haute" spot has added an extra dimension to its restaurant/nightclub offerings, with the debut of LAVO Casino Club, where grand-opening night saw rapper Busta Rhymes joining celebrity host, actor Joe Manganiello, at the blackjack tables.

Mon Ami Gabi (see page 168)

With perfect views of the Bellagio Fountains, this French bistro overlooking the Strip remains among my top picks for observing the herd on the street.

MR CHOW (see "Close, But No Cigar" page 131)

The seventh wonder from Michael Chow is where J. Lo chose to celebrate her opening night at Planet Hollywood, and is also where (show)room-mate Britney Spears' held her big New Year's Day bash.

Old Homestead Steakhouse (Caesars Palace)
(702) 731-7560

From DJ megastar Calvin Harris to actor Morgan Freeman, you never know who might be dining at this Las Vegas transplant of the historic New York original that claims to be the inventor of the doggy bag.

Sonny's Saloon
3449 Sammy Davis Jr Drive
(702) 731-5553

Sonny's claimed its place in infamy as the ransom-drop-off location in the 1993 kidnapping of Steve Wynn's daughter. Known back then as a hangout for off-shift casino employees, not much has changed; the customers start pouring in around 11 p.m., with a mix of old-timers, dealers, dancers, and other working types who make for some amazing only-in-Vegas people-watching.

STK Las Vegas (Cosmopolitan)
(702) 698-7990

From Tony Romo and Andre Agassi to Halle Berry and Jessica Alba, via Robin Thicke and Dan Aykroyd, the steakhouse at Cosmo can certainly boast some star-studded carnivores among its clientele.

TAO Asian Bistro (Venetian/Grand Canal Shoppes)
(702) 388-8338

If gossip-maven Perez Hilton chooses to dine here when he's in town, you know his likely won't be the only famous face in the house.

Additional Recommendations

VEGAN BUTTERNUT SQUASH VELOUTÉ
WITH ORGANIC ASIAN MUSHROOMS AND COFFEE FOAM AT EATT

SPECIAL DIET

CRUSH (see page 213)

Special diets must be cool, because this celebrity hotspot at MGM Grand caters to almost all of them: vegetarian, vegan, gluten-free, dairy-free, and seafood/shellfish-free options.

EATT Gourmet Bistro (Essential 52; see page 42)

French cuisine with a health-conscious spin.

Komol Restaurant
953 E. Sahara Avenue E-10
(702) 731-6542

A huge MSG-free Thai menu composed entirely of vegan and vegetarian options.

Lazeez Indian-Mediterranean Grill
8560 W. Desert Inn Road, #D-3
(702) 778-1613

This Indian-Middle Eastern halal grill serves a menu that includes an array of vegan, vegetarian, and gluten-free options.

Mint Indian Bistro (2 locations)
730 E. Flamingo Road / 4246 S. Durango
(702) 894-9334 / (702) 247-4610

One of Las Vegas' top Indian restaurants, Mint caters to a variety of special-diet needs, including vegan, vegetarian, and gluten-free, separate vegan and vegetarian versions of the chef's tasting menu, and a good lunch buffet; this is also the place for organic/vegan wine.

VegeNation (see page 159)

Open for breakfast through dinner, this downtown eatery is 100% plant-based and seasoned with their own herbs; there are also a dedicated kids' menu and a full bar that uses cold-pressed juices. Gluten-free dishes are marked on the menu.

Additional Recommendations

Veggie House (see page 144)

Violette's Vegan Organic Café & Juice Bar
8560 W. Desert Inn Road
(702) 685-0466

Veggie-laden creations and smoothies galore. The Violette is Cyndy Violette, one of the original "poker babes" and a World Series of Poker bracelet winner (2004).

Wynn/Encore

Every Wynn Resorts restaurant offers a "secret" veggie-friendly menu. You will need to ask your server to see it. Also noteworthy, the Buffet at Wynn is renowned for its sugar-free dessert options.

John Curtas

GRAPE EXPECTATIONS
(LAS VEGAS' BEST WINE DRINKING)

Las Vegas isn't really a "wine bar" sort of town. Wine bars generally require a certain level of introspection and contemplation and Las Vegas generally is about as contemplative as a UFC cage match. But this doesn't mean there aren't fabulous places to indulge your taste for fermented grapes. What it does mean is that you have to go to some of our finer restaurants to find wines (by the glass or bottle) that will blow your socks off.

Below are my 10 favorite sipping venues, places where our town's great sommeliers take enormous pride in pouring vintages from around the globe—wines you can drink, or think about, to your palate's content.

Estiatorio Milos

Greek wines may be unpronounceable, but they're delicious. They're also substantially underpriced compared to similar seafood-friendly wines from France and Italy. Don't even try to master the odd lisps and tongue rolls of Assyrtiko, Moshofilero, or Mavrodaphne.

Just point and smile, or ask the staff for help. (I promise they won't make fun of you.) Anyone who orders anything but Greek wines with this food should be sentenced to a year of drinking Harvey Wallbangers.

Restaurant Guy Savoy

The list is as thick as a dictionary and, at first blush, not for the faint of heart or parsimonious of purse. But look closely and you'll find a surprising number of bargains for less than $100. Or ask sommelier Phil Park and he'll happily point them out to you. The champagne bar is where you'll find serious oenophiles perusing the list a full half-hour before their reservation, just like they do it in France.

Marché Bacchus

A pinot noir wall, lakeside dining, and the gentlest mark-ups in town ($10 over retail) make MB a must-stop on any wine-lover's tour of Vegas. Jeff and Rhonda Wyatt are always there to help you choose

Additional Recommendations

a glass or a case of whatever mainstream cab or off-beat syrah suits your fancy. Or do what I do: Just stick with Burgundy and go nuts.

Ferraro's Italian Restaurant & Wine Bar

What I love about Italian wines is what I love about Italians and Italian food: They're friendly, passionate, fiercely regional, and confusing in a good way. Don't know your Montelcinos from your Montepulcianos? *Nessun problema.* Geno Ferraro is always there to help you parse the Barbarescos from the Barolos. One of the greatest Italian lists in America is at one of our finest Italian restaurants.

Bazaar Meat

I don't understand Spanish wine any more than I understand how José Andrés can have so much energy and so many great restaurants. But the next best thing to knowing a lot about a country's wines is knowing a sommelier who is eager to teach you. In Las Vegas, Chloe Helfand is that gal. She's always there with a smile and a lip-smacking wine you don't know made with a grape you've never heard of. Which is one of the reasons we love sommeliers. And Chloe.

La Cave

Mark Hefter's wine program is a lot like Mark Hefter: fun, interesting, intelligent, and all over the map. Hefter has poured wine from Le Cirque 2000 in New York to Spago and Circo in Las Vegas and needless to say, the man knows his grapes. With over 50 wines by the glass, he can dazzle anyone, from the novice drinker to the dedicated oenophile. But what we love about his list is its eclecticism.

At La Cave, you can dip your toe into the world's most interesting wines at very friendly price points. Curious about those orange and pink wines that are all the rage these days? Here's where to start.

Lotus of Siam

Robert Parker (yeah, that Robert Parker) calls Lotus' wine card the greatest for German wines in America and we have no reason to argue with him. It's also shoulder-deep in sake, Alsatian whites, and Austrian Grüner Veltliners—all of which match (in surprising ways) Saipan Chutima's fierce and fiery country-Thai cooking. This

John Curtas

is where you'll find almost every wine professional in town on their day off, usually at a table groaning with bottles of Riesling.

Sage

The trouble with Sage is that the food is so good, sometimes you forget about the wine, and the wine list is so good, sometimes you forget about the food. I like California pinot noir and chardonnay with Shawn McClain's innovative fare, but the list covers the world in all areas of consequence. Such choices here are a happy conundrum to experience, whether you're dining or hanging out in the stunning bar.

Mordeo Boutique Wine Bar

Small, well-chosen, and reasonably priced wine lists have popped up all over town in the past few years. Luis de Santos curates one of the best, full of bottles from around the world that go wonderfully with the eclectic menu. Half-price Mondays are an oenophiles dream.

Lamaii

A lion of a wine list in sheep's clothing—in this case, appended to a tasty Thai menu that gives no hint of the bargain bottles lurking nearby. The German Rieslings and French Chenin Blancs might go best with the food, but the Burgundies are where the bargains really lie.

WINE SELECTION AT LA CAVE

Epilogue

So there you have it, my tour of the greatest restaurants in one of the best restaurant cities on Earth, along with the best advice I can give about how to enjoy yourself when you're dining out.

It's been quite a ride these past 25 years. I've weathered divorce, substance abuse, and failures both professional and personal. Through it all, I've had the restaurants of Las Vegas to soothe my soul and keep me company. Through thousands of meals, a smiling hostess, a solicitous waiter, and fabulous food and drink have always consoled me. For years, through many of those trying times, the only thing that kept me going (and, to be frank, kept me in Las Vegas) were the wonderful meals waiting for me a short drive from my house. Not a day goes by that I'm not hungry for what this crazy town has to feed me. I can only hope you enjoy "eating Las Vegas" as much as I have.

MANDALAY BAY
MGM
BALLYS
THE MIRAG
CASINO & RESOR
BEATLES
LOVE
CIRQUE DU SOLEIL
JET

Section III

Index and Maps

Essential 52 Restaurants Index
(Casino Locations)

Essential 52 Restaurants Index
(Non-Casino Locations by nearest major cross streets)

All Restaurants Index

John Curtas

All Restaurants Index

All Restaurants Index

John Curtas

All Restaurants Index

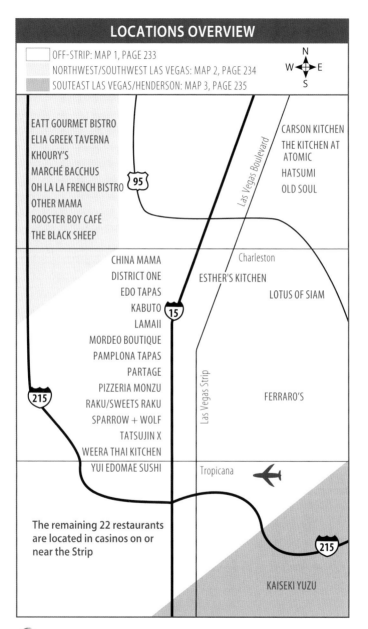

LOCATIONS OVERVIEW

OFF-STRIP: MAP 1, PAGE 233
NORTHWEST/SOUTHWEST LAS VEGAS: MAP 2, PAGE 234
SOUTEAST LAS VEGAS/HENDERSON: MAP 3, PAGE 235

N
W + E
S

EATT GOURMET BISTRO
ELIA GREEK TAVERNA
KHOURY'S
MARCHÉ BACCHUS
OH LA LA FRENCH BISTRO
OTHER MAMA
ROOSTER BOY CAFÉ
THE BLACK SHEEP

95

Las Vegas Boulevard

CARSON KITCHEN
THE KITCHEN AT
ATOMIC
HATSUMI
OLD SOUL

CHINA MAMA
DISTRICT ONE
EDO TAPAS
KABUTO
LAMAII
MORDEO BOUTIQUE
PAMPLONA TAPAS
PARTAGE
PIZZERIA MONZU
RAKU/SWEETS RAKU
SPARROW + WOLF
TATSUJIN X
WEERA THAI KITCHEN
YUI EDOMAE SUSHI

Charleston

ESTHER'S KITCHEN

LOTUS OF SIAM

15

Las Vegas Strip

FERRARO'S

Tropicana

The remaining 22 restaurants
are located in casinos on or
near the Strip

215

215

KAISEKI YUZU

John Curtas

OFF-STRIP, MAP 1

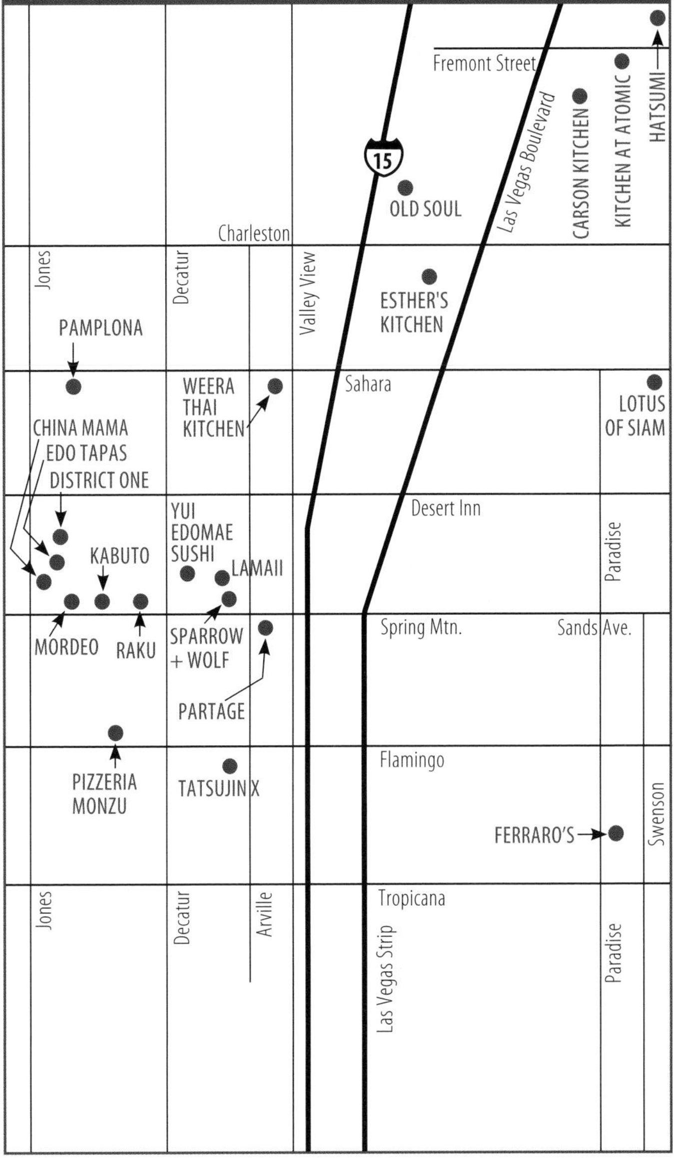

HATSUMI

KITCHEN AT ATOMIC

CARSON KITCHEN

Las Vegas Boulevard

Fremont Street

15

OLD SOUL

Charleston

Jones

Decatur

Valley View

ESTHER'S KITCHEN

PAMPLONA

WEERA THAI KITCHEN

Sahara

LOTUS OF SIAM

CHINA MAMA
EDO TAPAS
DISTRICT ONE

YUI EDOMAE SUSHI

LAMAII

Desert Inn

Paradise

KABUTO

MORDEO   RAKU

SPARROW + WOLF

Spring Mtn.

Sands Ave.

PARTAGE

PIZZERIA MONZU

TATSUJIN X

Flamingo

FERRARO'S

Swenson

Jones

Decatur

Arville

Tropicana

Las Vegas Strip

Paradise

NORTHWEST/SOUTHWEST LAS VEGAS, MAP 2

Cheyenne

MARCHÉ BACCHUS

Regatta

Smoke Ranch

ROOSTER BOY CAFÉ

Rampart

Lake Mead Blvd

❷
❸

OH LA LA FRENCH BISTRO

159

❶
← 3 MILES

Charleston

Hualapai Way

← KHOURY'S

Fort Apache

Durango

Cimarron

Buffalo

Rainbow

Town Center Drive

Sahara

EATT GOURMENT BISTRO

Desert Inn

Spring Mtn. Rd

OTHER MAMA

Flamingo

ELIA GREEK TAVERNA

Patrick Lane

215

THE BLACK SHEEP

Warm Springs

Teneya Way

NEARBY CASINOS: ❶ RED ROCK RESORT, ❷ RAMPART, ❸ SUNCOAST

John Curtas

Sunset

Warm Springs

Windmill

Wigwam

Maryland Parkway

Eastern

Pecos

Green Valley Parkway

KAISEKI YUZU

Silverado Ranch Blvd.

215

❷

St. Rose Parkway

❶

6 MILES

Sunridge Heights Parkway

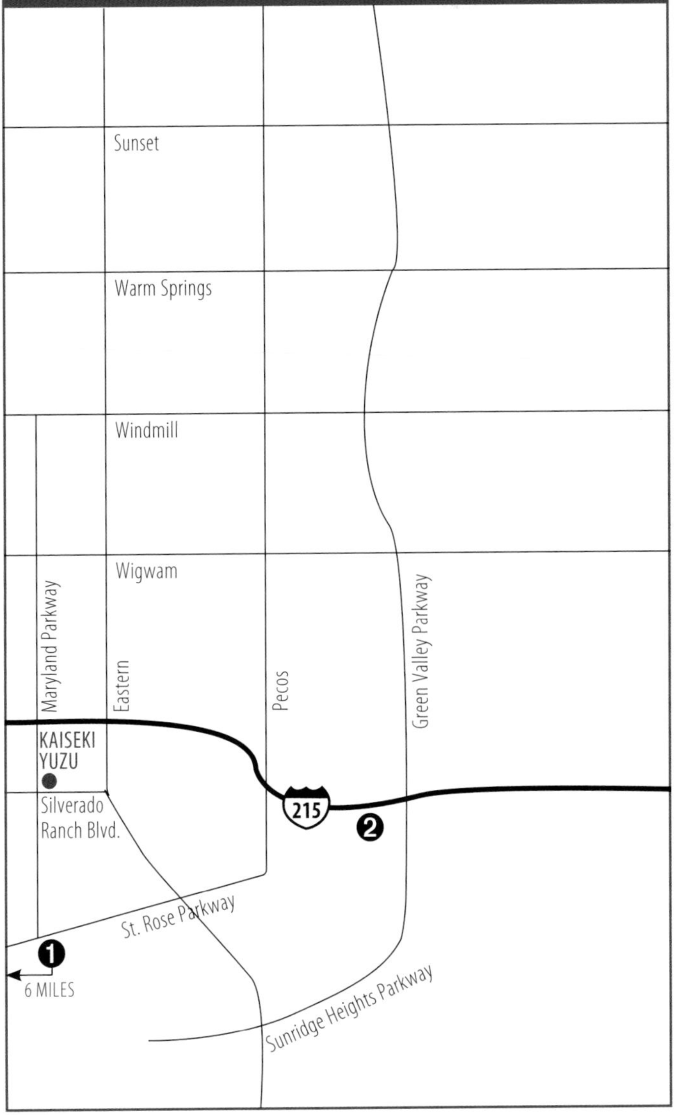

NEARBY CASINOS: ❶ M RESORT, ❷ GREEN VALLEY RANCH

About the Author

JOHN CURTAS has been covering the Las Vegas food and restaurant scene since 1995. His "Food For Thought" commentaries ran for 15 years on KNPR Nevada Public Radio, and these days he can be seen every Friday as Las Vegas' "Favorite Foodie" on KSNV's (NBC) Channel 3's "Wake Up With the Wagners." He has written reviews for more magazines and guidebooks than he can count and has appeared multiple times as a judge on "Iron Chef America" and "Top Chef Masters." In addition, he authors the Eating Las Vegas food blog (www.eatinglv.com). This seventh edition of Eating Las Vegas reflects his 32 years of eating in more restaurants, more often, than anyone in the history of Las Vegas.

About Huntington Press

Huntington Press is a specialty publisher of Las Vegas- and gambling-related books and periodicals, including the award-winning consumer newsletter, *Anthony Curtis' Las Vegas Advisor.*

Huntington Press
3665 Procyon Street
Las Vegas, Nevada 89103
LasVegasAdvisor.com
books@huntingtonpress.com